Sue and Ed,

Happy Birthday (Sue)
    Happy Anniversary
to my special friend
with whom many
cherished memories
have been made.

                Love,
                Mary Ann
                July 2009

EATING *Royally*

DARREN MCGRADY

THOMAS NELSON
Since 1798

NASHVILLE   DALLAS   MEXICO CITY   RIO DE JANEIRO   BEIJING

I dedicate this book to the memory of two special ladies: To my Nan Florrie Lambert who meant so much to me and would have been so proud of this book, it would have been shown all around the bingo hall. And of course to Princess Diana, who taught me to be humble and made me realize that while charity work can be hard, it is the most satisfying, and that giving is so much more rewarding than taking.

Published in Nashville, Tennessee. Thomas Nelson is a trademark of Thomas Nelson, Inc.

Food photography by Leonardo Frusteri.

Page design by Walter Petrie.

Thomas Nelson, Inc. titles may be purchased in bulk for educational, business, fund-raising, or sales promotional use. For information, please e-mail SpecialMarkets@ThomasNelson.com.

Library of Congress Cataloging-in-Publication Data

McGrady, Darren, 1962–
   Eating royally / Darren McGrady.
     p. cm.
   Includes index.
   ISBN-13: 978-1-4016-0321-2
   ISBN-10: 1-4016-0321-1
   1. McGrady, Darren, 1962— 2. Cooks—England—Biography.
3. Windsor, House of. I. Title.
TX649.M44A3 2007
641.5092—dc22

[B]   2007001358

Printed in Singapore

07 08 09 10 11 TWP 5 4 3 2

Table of Contents

Preface

It was while traveling around the country raising money to promote breast cancer awareness that I decided to write this book. People were fascinated by the little anecdotes I told and the food I prepared, and they wanted more. And so this book was born. It was only fitting, then, that my advance from this book should therefore go to charity. I chose the Elizabeth Glaser Pediatric AIDS Foundation because it linked two of Princess Diana's charitable goals—children and AIDS. I wanted it to be a book that William and Harry could show to their children and say, "Look, this is what Granny Diana used to eat when we were your age."

Thank you to Catherine Drayton—my literary agent until I scared her back to Australia—for believing there could be a good book here. I owe you an ice cream. To Alexis Hurley and Eleanor Jackson of Inkwell Management for picking up the project reigns and guiding it to fruition. Thank you both for your patience, support, advice, direction, and for convincing me that you can't write a book in two weeks. You are the best! Thanks to all at Thomas Nelson for creating a beautiful book, especially to Pamela Clements for having faith in the project, and to Geoffrey Stone and Lori Jones for their leadership and talent and for humoring me and accommodating my requests as often as possible. Enormous thanks to Susan Ruffins for her endurance and discipline in keeping me on track and on time. Without you I would still be on the first chapter. Thank you for writing me exactly as I speak. You have such talent and humor and I am proud to have worked with you.

A huge thank you to Mr. and Mrs. Charles Wyly Jr. for their support and kindness over the four years it took to put this book together. Special thanks to

Jill Rowlett and Lee Bailey for the stunning English antique silver and china in the food shots and who, along with Yvonne Crum, knew everyone when it came to "borrowing" the best props and equipment. To Abigail Davies and Eddie Dennis at Neiman Marcus for the best selection of English china and crystal. To Terry Van Wilson and Angela Malone of Porthault for the finest linen outside Buckingham Palace. To Charles and Nell Roberts of London Market antiques for adding the British history to the food shots and helping make them authentic. To Leo Frusteri for turning my food into works of art, *bellissimo*! Leo, you are a star.

Most importantly, I want to thank my wife, Wendy, who had to put up with many weekends, late nights, and holidays when I was at the computer or test-ing recipes. I love you and couldn't have done this without your support and encouragement. And to Kelly, Lexie, and Harry, who told me many times to "ask Miss Alexis if you can have a day off, Dad." Well, now I can. To my mother Pauline who inspired me with her own cooking and to my father Michael who kept digging deep into his pocket while I was learning. Also to my siblings Chris and Sacha. Thank you all for supporting me, believing in me, and giving me the confidence to face any challenge.

— Darren McGrady

Warmest thanks to Alexis Hurley and Eleanor Jackson at Inkwell Management for offering me space in the kitchen and at the table! I will always be grateful. Thanks to all the folks at Thomas Nelson Publishers including Geoffrey Stone, Pamela Clements, and Lori Jones. Your guidance, speed, and editorial generosity are deeply appreciated. Special thank you to Darren, whose stamina in slogging through draft upon draft ensured that we got it just right and whose kindness, good spirits, and graceful nature made work feel like play.

Thank you to Seth, Theo, and Olivia for your tremendous understanding and patience. This could not have happened without your support. I love you all more than I can ever express. A final thank you to Margaret Giganti, whose talent, love, and wisdom was given to me without reserve. It nourishes me still.

— Susan Ruffins

Opening

How do you become a chef to the British royal family? It's seems as if I've just been terribly lucky and, in fact, that certainly plays a part. But after twenty-five years in kitchens both grand and modest, I remain passionate about food and cooking. And at no time more than when I was cooking for the royal family.

I began cooking at Buckingham Palace shortly after the marriage of Lady Diana and Prince Charles and remained in royal service until the death of Princess Diana in 1997. During that time I rose to senior pastry chef at the palace and then to the prestigious position of Princess Diana's private chef at Kensington Palace. My fifteen years working for the royal family were key in helping me master my métier. But the experience was ultimately much more than just excellent training—it formed the person I am today. I remember it all with great affection, and with Princess Diana's death, also a tinge of sadness. This book is written with two goals in mind: to share what I have learned and to set down my memories in print.

Today, as in the past, the word *royalty* connotes an anointed life, separate and apart from the lives of everyday people. But my experience working for the Windsors was just the opposite. In fact, the royal family, with their traditions and sense of service, made me feel British to the core. And underneath all the external trappings of modern royal life, the royal household is really just a home for a large, extended family with its daily routines, styles, and tastes. Make no mistake, their household, like yours, has its quirks. But what may seem quirky at the outset often has a historical and symbolic underpinning. Learning this made my work as a chef all the richer.

It seems fitting in a way that this book's arrival coincides so closely with

Queen Elizabeth's eightieth birthday and the tenth anniversary of Princess Diana's passing. Both of these women affected the path of my life in ways I could never have foreseen. Both deeply impressed me with the notion that although life may include personal passions and interests, it is fundamentally about service toward others. This has been an essential lesson in my work as a chef, and I am grateful to have the opportunity to share my knowledge with others.

When I think back, I realize that my becoming a chef was perhaps pre-ordained. Growing up in Newark, England, food was quite important, not only as a source of pleasure, but also as a source of income. My mum and dad both worked outside the home, my mum as a chef in a local hotel in Nottinghamshire. When your mum is a chef, you learn not to be a fussy eater. Food at home was quite a bit more eclectic than in most British households in the seventies. My sister, brother, and I were introduced at an early age to not only excellent traditional British cooking, but also to French and Italian food. But, I didn't actually cook much as a child. Instead I was an avid eater.

The real reason I started cooking began in high school. I signed up for a "domestic science" course (in the US it would be called home economics). The best part of it all was that you got to eat what you made! It was a superb situation for a growing boy of fifteen who was constantly hungry.

I learned all sorts of things, including some not on the syllabus. I made pastry dough for tarts and also found out that if you eat jam tarts straight from the oven it will result in excruciating pain as the hot sugar adheres to the top of your mouth. I enjoyed it all and proudly showed off my newfound skills to my family. My mum, who has always enjoyed a life around food, encouraged my early attempts. I think she knew that I would enjoy cooking.

I had always been a hands-on student, excelling in subjects that allowed me to translate academic ideas via a physical experience. In school, cooking classes were one of the few places where such an approach to learning was acceptable. Otherwise school was quite traditionally bookish and I often struggled. Both my parents, bless them, understood that I didn't have much of an academic nature. The thought of going on to university after high school was daunting for me. So, with my mum's encouragement, I decided to attend a two-year catering college after graduating from high school at sixteen. The college was about twenty minutes from home, and best of all, it was free.

At the same time, my mum thought a little practical experience was in order. The summer before I started college she got me a job as a dishwasher at the hotel where she worked. John Berry, a wonderful fellow who ran the place, hired me. As you can imagine, the dishwasher occupies the lowest rung in any professional kitchen, and I was to start from the bottom up.

My strategy was to get all the dirty dishes done early in my shift and then to spend the rest of the time watching all the chefs do their work. It was a fascinating place. It was a classic hotel kitchen, which means it was very well set up. There was a cold station, where all the salads, sandwiches, and other cold buffet dishes were prepared. Then there was a sauce station, fish station, and meat station. I rotated myself through the kitchen, always standing behind the chefs, trying not to get in anyone's way and keeping my eyes open. I didn't win any awards for excellent dishwashing, but I did my job well and enjoyed being in a professional kitchen. It was a wonderful introduction.

That summer experience gave me a lead over all the other students when I started college in the fall. I was one of the few students who had worked in a professional kitchen. I certainly needed training, though, and my first year was extremely busy with new lessons. I worked hard, and the year seemed to fly by.

Mr. Berry and I had kept up an intermittent correspondence during the course of the year. He had left the hotel in Nottinghamshire and moved to Ballathie House Hotel, a seventeenth-century country house in Perthshire, overlooking the River Tay in Scotland. At the end of my first year, he invited me to Scotland to work for the summer. He thought I showed promise and knew I could work hard. I was excited to travel for the summer and to move up from dishwashing!

After all these years I still recall how wonderful that summer was for me. I had never seen ingredients like this before. Nothing from a can! Gorgeous whole salmon that we would cook, smoke, or brine. Wild grouse and all sorts of local birds. Game in abundance. What a luxurious experience for a kid of seventeen! I worked my tail off that summer, and I reckon Mr. Berry got his money's worth out of me.

I started to gain confidence in the kitchen and returned to school in the fall ready to put all my experience to good use. It did indeed pay off. I quickly moved through the ranks of my classmates and graduated at the top of my class.

One of my teachers, who had been especially pessimistic about my prospects when I started college, was quite surprised at how well I performed. I wonder what she would think now if she learned that I went on to cook for the Queen of England and Princess Diana!

Though many of my classmates were perfectly content to remain close to home, I knew I didn't want to stay in Newark as a local chef. My experience in Scotland had definitely piqued my interest in learning what the outside world could offer. But where should I go? London, of course!

My mum and dad were, as always, supportive, although I expect my dad wasn't too pleased at the cost of setting his son up in London. Nor were my brother and sister thrilled when they considered how my career dreams might be siphoning off funds which, no doubt, they could have put to good use. My grandmother was quite convinced that I was heading toward danger. After all, an eighteen-year-old lad on his own in London would clearly come to no good. No good at all.

In the restaurant kitchen at the Savoy

The one stipulation from both my parents was that I needed to have at least the inkling of a job before I left. Initially I considered applying for a job in the Royal Air Force. A good friend, Pete Males, spoke highly of his military cooking experience. He had retired as a warrant officer and came to Clarendon College as a lecturer to finish his career. But it is the RAF and you do have to go through basic training. Plus, the commitment was a whopping fifteen years. I just wasn't quite ready for that.

The other possibility was hotel work. I had some experience, of course. And in the year I graduated, 1980, the most elegant food was still being served in hotels in London. I applied for positions with both the Waldorf Hotel and the Savoy. I was accepted at both and decided on the Savoy. I traveled off to London confident that I could handle myself in any culinary situation.

By day two, my confidence had evaporated. There were seventy chefs in the kitchen, and I was the last fellow on the list. How could I have been so puffed up? I knew nothing! At least that was how I felt. The first week I just watched the chefs and quaked in my boots. Then I went back to my little rented room and cried.

While the Savoy Hotel was—and remains—a glamorous place, the Savoy kitchen was straight out of Victorian England. There were actually coal ovens at some stations. Pakistani kitchen helpers would come in with huge buckets of coal and fire up the ovens. Temperature control was limited. There was no air-conditioning, and it was a blazingly hot kitchen to work in during the summer months and only tolerably warm in the winter.

The chefs ranged in age from eighteen to thirty-five and many came from France or Germany. It wasn't uncommon for fistfights to break out among competitive chefs. The days were long. Fifteen- to eighteen-hour shifts were the norm, and there were many times I collapsed on the subway after my shift and missed my stop. I had never been so tired in my life.

A bleary-eyed McGrady family after sleeping overnight on the Mall. Brother Chris is taking the photo.

In my two years at the Savoy I rotated through a number of stations and advanced to a position just below chef de Partie. It was a thoroughly exhausting and exhilarating experience. Many of the chefs I worked with remain good friends to this day. But we all moved on. You simply could not remain at the Savoy a long time. Burnout was inevitable.

Toward the end of my second year, London was frantically busy primping for a royal wedding. In 1982 Prince Charles wed Lady Diana Spencer in one of the most lavish royal weddings in history. My mum was quite fond of the royal family, and she and my dad decided to come down to London and camp out on the Mall in hopes of getting a glimpse of Lady Di. I joined them. I was already thinking of moving out of the Savoy kitchens and considering my next step. As I watched the royal entourage pass on its way to St. Paul's Cathedral I wondered how a new address would look on my resume. Buckingham Palace, for example?

A Royal Introduction

In England, to get a job working for the Queen carries a certain cachet even today and, as a result, is highly sought after and quite competitive. I was lucky in having close ties with a former chef mate from the Savoy who had moved up to Buckingham Palace. Not too long after the royal wedding of Prince Charles and Lady Diana Spencer, chef Mark Fromont invited me in for a chat and a look around the kitchens. I very much liked what I saw. I thought about how interesting it would be to cook for kings and queens and the royal family. So, with a bit of bravado, I sent a letter expressing my interest in working at Buckingham Palace to the assistant master of the household, Mr. Michael Parker.

Soon afterward, I received a letter stamped with the royal crest, granting me an interview the following week. Well, I felt very important the morning of my interview when asked "Where to?" by the cabbie and being able to say, "Buckingham Palace, side-door entrance please."

I was directed into the left ground-floor side of the palace and into the office of Mr. Parker, a very proper gentleman with a quintessential upper class British accent. He was very detailed in his questions about my background and skills, but since Mr. Parker had also come from the Savoy, he already knew a great deal about my training.

I received an offer as junior cook and went to work at Buckingham Palace several weeks later.

Working at Buckingham Palace is a "live in" job. There are wings of dormitory-style rooms for single men and single women in the palace and larger apartments in the Royal Mews for employees with families. Staff was also housed on the grounds of Windsor Castle and Hampton Court. The children who grow up within the palace walls often become palace employees. The royal family embraces a socially democratic relationship with its employees, providing housing, health care, clothing, six weeks of vacation, and loyal long-term employment. The joke is that you work at Buckingham Palace either ten minutes or forty years. The drawback to all this is that the pay is pretty lousy. No matter, I was thrilled.

During the next eleven years I worked for the Queen and traveled around the world twice as part of my job. I saw the US, Australia, New Zealand, Nepal, France, Italy, Cypress, and the Channel Islands. I spent extensive periods at other royal residences in England, including Balmoral and Sandringham. I had the unique opportunity to participate in a life that—while certainly modern—still carries with it a recognizable link to traditions spanning one thousand years.

The royal calendar is still set around the seasons and traditions established through time and by successive monarchies. There are the summer months at Balmoral, Christmas at Sandringham, annual balls and charity events at Buckingham Palace, sailing on the HMY *Britannia*, state visits, and garden parties. The royal family still eats seasonally and with much of the food sourced from its own significant land holdings. They are devoted to game caught on the grounds, berries picked from their own bushes, and dairy products from their own herds.

The royal calendar also details the Queen's movements throughout the year. She and the rest of the royal family are at various times in residence at Buckingham Palace, Sandringham Castle, Windsor Castle, and Balmoral Castle with additional trips to Scotland and on the royal yacht.

This all makes for staffing challenges. Because the royal family moves from place to place so often, there are households to open and close up, shipments of provisions from one castle or country to the next, and personnel traveling to and fro all the time. But all this movement of people and goods has been honed down to a science.

Buckingham Palace is not just the official London residence of the Queen and the royal entourage, but is also the administrative headquarters of the monarchy. So the full workings of the royal family and the monarchy's activities in the UK and abroad are coordinated through the palace with quite a military level of precision.

That air of precision extends to every aspect of managing the royal household. Two weeks after I began working, I was sent from London to Balmoral Castle where the royal family was vacationing. I was prepping vegetables when the head chef came over and said, "Right. Now let me show you how to prepare the Queen's carrots." He then took three very large carrots, peeled, trimmed, and topped them. He sliced them lengthwise and in half so each carrot was of equal length. The carrots were then placed in a white paper bag and the bag was folded shut. "There," he said. "That is how you do it."

"But Chef," I asked, now totally bewildered, "aren't they a bit large and don't we need to cook them?"

"Large?" His eyebrows shot up. "Of course not. They'll be fine for the horses. And don't ever cut them any shorter than that or she will blame us when the damn horse bites her fingers."

The Queen's footman—or "dog boy" as he was known around the palace—picked up the carrots from the kitchen and placed them in a pocket of the Queen's riding coat. After each ride, she would feed them to her horse. I think it is safe to say that the Queen's horses have no idea that carrots have a skin.

This regimented approach took getting used to. Cooking is a creative endeavor, and most chefs chafe at making the same dish over and over again unchanged. I made thousands of scones during my time with the royal family, and I had to make sure that each batch was exactly like the last one. To be a successful palace chef you must bring that professional discipline to the job whether cooking a single dinner for the Queen, an elegant multicourse dinner for a hundred, or alas, as I did many times, a midmorning snack for the horses.

ROYAL TEA SCONES

Scones were part of the Queen's daily tea service. They were served religiously each day, alternating between fruit scones or plain scones. This routine was so fixed that each Monday morning the head chef would call the senior weekend chef to find out what "flavor" to make, either fruit or plain.

While the Queen insisted on them as part of her tea, I suspect she didn't actually like scones. I say that because she never, ever, ate them. Instead, at the end of her daily tea, the Queen would take a scone and crumble it onto the floor for the corgis. It seems the dogs quite liked them.

Don't be put off though. These scones are really, really good. Served warm with lots of butter. they make an absolutely tender, crumbly treat. When they cool, split them in half and fill with strawberry preserves, clotted cream, or whipped cream. You will have no problem polishing them off.

3¼ cups all-purpose flour	1 egg, beaten
½ cup plus 1 tablespoon extra-fine granulated sugar	¾ cup to 1¼ cups milk
4 teaspoons baking powder	1 cup raisins (optional)
1 stick (½ cup) unsalted butter, softened	1 beaten egg yolk for glazing

1. Preheat the oven to 350 degrees. Combine the flour, sugar, and baking powder in a large bowl. Cut in the butter and stir until the flour mixture resembles fine bread crumbs. Make a well in the center of the mixture, and add the beaten egg and about ¾ cup of milk. Add the raisins now if making a fruit scone. Bring the mixture together with a metal spoon, making sure you don't overmix and toughen the dough. If the mixture seems dry and crumbly, add more of the remaining milk, but add it gradually. You want lightly bound dough that is neither too wet nor too dry.

2. Lightly dust a cutting board with flour, and roll out the dough to about 1 inch thick. Then, using a 2-inch round cookie cutter, cut out about 16 scones and place them on an ungreased baking sheet about 1 inch apart. Brush the tops of the scones with the beaten egg yolk.

3. Bake for 15 to 20 minutes, or until scones are lightly colored. Serve hot or transfer scones to a cooling rack.

MAKES 16 SCONES

CHAPTER ONE

The Royal Year

The royal calendar is set a year in advance and is quite detailed. This level of advance planning is only possible because there are certain activities that are repeated year after year by the Queen and the royal family. In broad strokes, a standard calendar looks like this:

Late December until early February: Christmas and the New Year at
Sandringham Castle

February: State visits in late February. During the third week a
state banquet for one hundred fifty people is held at
Buckingham Palace.

March to mid-May: Windsor Castle. The Queen's birthday is April
21 and is always celebrated at Windsor, as is the Easter holiday.
The Royal Windsor Horse Show is held during the second week
of May.

Late May to mid-June: Buckingham Palace. The Queen attends to
affairs of state, including investitures and state visits. In May, the
Chelsea flower show and the anniversary celebration of the
Queen's birthday are held. The Duke's birthday is on the tenth
of June.

Late June: Windsor Castle and a celebration of the Royal Ascot
horse races. Leaving Windsor Castle, the Queen spends the last
week of June in Edinburgh, Scotland, at Holyrood Palace. A
garden party and a thistle lunch are always on the schedule.

July: Garden parties at Buckingham Palace

Early August: Aboard HMY *Britannia* for regatta racing and sailing
among the Western Isles.

August until early October: Vacation at Balmoral Castle in the
highlands of Scotland

November: Buckingham Palace and a large annual reception for the
Diplomatic Corps with as many as fifteen hundred people in
attendance

Early December: Buckingham Palace for state visits and banquets

As a chef, I tend to associate the royal residences with seasons and food. I
think of Buckingham Palace as the workaday location during late fall and winter, as well as early summer. To me the palace conjures up images of hearty
stews, refined banquets, private lunches and dinner parties, and large summer
tea parties.

Sandringham means Christmas and English trifle, chocolate Yule log, pâtés,
and terrines. Sandringham also has a wonderful fruit farm with nearly seventy
acres of amazing apples—Laxtons Fortunes, Cox's, and Bramleys—which make
the best apple pies.

Windsor Castle is linked with the arrival of spring and early lettuces, peas,
asparagus, and rhubarb ready to harvest.

Balmoral is forever associated with high summer holidays, ice cream, and
berry picking. The gardens are full of raspberries, strawberries, gooseberries—red
and green—and frais de bois, which are little woodland strawberries that only
need a jug of heavy cream and a bowl of caster sugar to grace the royal tables.

MENU

Oeufs Drumkilbo

Suprême de Volaille en Croûte
Sauce au Citron Vert
Carottes et Petits Maïs au Beurre
Poireaux Glacés
Pommes Dauphine

Salade

———

Cornets de Glace Vanille

LES VINS
Rüdesheimer Magdalenenkreuz Kabinett
1983
Aloxe-Corton 1983
Royal Vintage 1955

MERCREDI, LE 21 MARS, 1990   BUCKINGHAM PALACE

Queen's menu

Pièces de Turbot Walewska

Tournedos Soubé Rossini

Salade

Mirabelles Flambées
Crème glacée

Mercredi le 25 Juillet 1984.

Queen Mother's menu

Timbale d'Epinards
Sauce Champignons
****
Poulet Poêlé aux Herbes
Petits Pois Flamande
Courgettes Pochées
Pommes Château
****
Salade d'Endives et d'Oranges
****
Crêpes Islandaise

Vendredi le 28 Juillet

Duke of Edinburgh's menu

Roulade d'épinards et champignons
à la mayonnaise parfumée aux truffes

• • •

Venaison braisée aux petites légumes

• • •

Diplomat pudding

Dîner   Samedi,
HM Yacht BRITANNIA   le 29 mai 1993

Prince Charles's menu

GOUJONS DE SAUMON
SAUCE VERTE

CARRE D'AGNEAU
AUX CHAMPIGNONS SAUVAGES

SALADE

CITRON PARFAIT MERINGUE
SAUCE FRAMBOISES

MARDI LE 19 MARS 1991

Prince Andrew's menu

KENSINGTON PALACE

Menu

Terrine de legumes,
coulis au poivres rouge

Fettuccine au Champignons Sauvage

Glace au Mangue et gingembre

Mercredi le 4 Juin 1997

KENSINGTON PALACE

Princess Dianna's menu

CHAPTER TWO

Buckingham Palace

Winter Balls and Summer Teas

Buckingham Palace is one of the world's most famous buildings. More than fifty thousand people walk through its doors each year to attend banquets, lunches, dinners, receptions, and royal garden parties. It is an official residence of Her Majesty, Queen Elizabeth II, and she spends about thirty weeks there each year.

It also is the central hub of royal administration, supporting the day-to-day activities and duties of the Queen and her family, no matter where they might be. The palace is the venue for many royal ceremonies, including state visits and investitures, and is used regularly by the Queen and family for official and state entertaining.

*The Lord Chamberlain is
commanded by Her Majesty to invite*

Mr. Darren McGrady
*to a Garden Party
at Buckingham Palace
on Thursday 25th July 1996 from 4 to 6 pm*

This card does not admit

The most active times at Buckingham Palace are late February and March, July, November, and the first part of December. In the summer the Queen hosts garden parties on the palace grounds and in the winter the palace becomes a glittering backdrop for state visits and receptions.

The chefs in the royal kitchens support all of this activity as well as the day-to-day feeding of the royal family and as many as three hundred full-time staff employees. Located on the ground floor, the kitchen has been modernized by Queen Elizabeth. While it's not the cutting-edge kitchen you would find in a top-notch hotel, it is certainly more than adequate to meet the palace's needs. As a result of modernizing the kitchen, the enormous number of cooks required during Queen Victoria's time (as many as sixty-five if it was a large state banquet) is no longer necessary.

Today, if the Queen is in residence, there are usually around ten chefs on duty in the royal kitchen. Not that she needs ten chefs to cook dinner for her. It is just that the number of staff and support personnel increases wherever the Queen goes and unfortunately they regularly get hungry. Buckingham Palace has a brigade of twenty chefs, and these chefs provide round-the-clock service at all of the royal residences throughout the country, or abroad, whenever a member of the royal family is in residence at that location. Like a hotel, Buckingham Palace never really closes.

On my way to hunt for wild mushrooms on Balmoral Castle grounds

The royal palate hasn't changed much even though England has grown more culturally diverse. Although the Princes William and Harry count pizza among their favorite foods, they also adore game, roasts, and typical British food such as cottage pie. Prince Charles is a very health-conscious eater and enjoys whole grains, organic vegetables, and simply prepared fish and meats. In fact, he once brought Antonio Carluccio, a well-known Italian cook in London, to Balmoral to search for and bottle wild mushrooms. Carluccio is well known as an amateur mycologist, and through him I learned to identify and use cèpes, known in Italy as "porcini mushrooms." I quickly understood what Prince Charles had known for a long time: Balmoral is an absolute treasure trove of wild mushrooms.

Unfortunately for Prince Charles, the Queen's head chef, Peter Page, also knew that cèpes grew abundantly on the property, and he was adamant the prince's chefs were not going to take them. He organized mushroom raids across the estate before Prince Charles's entourage arrived at Balmoral. The prince's chefs were more than a little irritated. *Oh well, chalk one up for the Queen's men,* I thought. We chopped mushrooms up to use in soup and used them as garnishes for all the wonderful game on the estate.

If I had to define the style of royal British cuisine, I would be forced to acknowledge that classical French influences are still very much in evidence, especially for state banquets and balls. This is partially because Queen Elizabeth has the final say on all menus, and the food at Buckingham Palace reflects her preferences.

From Kitchen to Table

Distances within the palace take some getting used to. In fact, the kitchen is located a full mile and a quarter away and several floors under the Queen's dining rooms. So, getting hot food to its final destination has always been an issue. The current method for transporting food from one end of the palace to the other is the use of heated trolleys that are rolled quickly from the kitchen to their final destination. The trolleys hold covered silver dishes outfitted with an extra water bath beneath to keep food warm.

It is the footmen's job to transport meals around the palace; they have their routes mapped out. For example, if they are delivering a meal to the Queen, the footmen will take an L-shaped route from the kitchen to the Queen's private elevator. This elevator is made available during mealtimes for the sole purpose of getting the food to her quickly.

Oddly enough, sometimes the food isn't all located in the same place. For example, if Prince Edward wants a simple meal of scrambled eggs and toast, the footman picks up the eggs made in the royal kitchen and then, about one hundred yards down the corridor, has to pick up the toast made in the coffee room kitchen. The military execution of it all would bring to mind a great Monty Python sketch.

Though meals at Buckingham Palace can be simple, the raw ingredients are always first rate. In addition to amazing game and fish, which the royal estates provide directly, the palace maintains special long-term relationships with purveyors who provide goods at a discounted price to the royal family in exchange for the "royal warrant." The royal warrant is the royal seal and can be exhibited directly on chosen purveyors' packaging. It's a great marketing tool.

One major purveyor is Hyams & Cockerton, who supplies fruit and vegetables for the royal family. They handpick produce for the palace and the quality is incredible. So good, in fact, that when the chefs have to pack up to travel to Balmoral or Sandringham, or even abroad, H & C produce is loaded along with our standard supplies. We shipped quite a lot of food to Balmoral in particular. Each day fresh supplies were dropped off at Buckingham Palace, checked by the chef on duty, and then readied for the nightly trip to Balmoral. The deliveries from London were a necessity. After all, you could never serve an unripe pear to the royal table.

What Will the Queen Eat?

While the Queen does have the final say on what she wants to eat, she doesn't spend her time scribbling up menus and shopping lists! When I was at Buckingham Palace, Chef Page, the head chef at the time, would develop a list of menu suggestions each day to present to the Queen for her approval. Page, a portly man who liked a drink or two, was an endless font of information and talent. He had served the Queen for more than forty years and was one of the very few staff that the Queen would call by first name.

Each day he would write his suggestions down in a red leather-bound book with "Menu Royal" embossed in gold on the cover. As soon as one book was filled, it was sent to the royal archives and a new book was sent to the kitchen as a replacement. When I was the chef for Princess Diana at Kensington Palace, I intended to continue the "Menu Royal" tradition. After all, she had a menu book—all of the royals did—until she and Prince Charles separated. Princess Diana, however, objected. She thought it was a waste of money and asked, "Why would anyone in years to come want to know what I ate?" Instead I kept plain, cheap notebooks for my files and to this day I have held on to the last one.

DAY-TO-DAY LIFE

Queen Elizabeth really treats Buckingham Palace as "the office" and spends most of her time there as a duty rather than by choice. It is clear that she can't wait for Friday afternoon when she can head off to Windsor Castle for the weekend.

At Buckingham Palace, the daily routine for meals is set: breakfast at 9:00 a.m., lunch promptly at 1:15 p.m., tea at 5:00 p.m., and dinner at 8:15 p.m. Breakfast is almost no work for a palace chef as the Queen is quite happy with tea and toast. Lunch and dinner are more elaborate, especially if guests are invited in.

Cooking meals for royalty, even simple meals, connotes a high standard of preparation and service. Even if I had to make a simple cold lunch, it still needed to be gracefully and beautifully presented. A good example was a popular first course dish of tomato and dill mousse with lobster. Princess Diana routinely requested it, and it was as delicious as it was elegant. The recipe is enriched with sour cream, heavy cream, and mayonnaise. When I moved across to Kensington Palace as Diana's chef, this mousse was one of the first recipes I reworked into a nonfat version. Both are good.

Who Foots the Bill?

The cost of the monarchy is borne by the state. So, while royal entertaining may be lavish, the day-to-day royal meals for family and staff are quite simple. This trend toward simpler meals is partly a reflection of contemporary British society, but is also influenced by economics. Truth be told, the modern royal family is on a budget. The cost of maintaining the monarchy was roughly one dollar per British citizen last year. That is a great "deal" for the British if you consider how many tourists come to England to see Buckingham Palace, Windsor Castle, and other royal attractions. The monarchy today brings in significant tourism and a lot of cash.

The royal family loved all types of fish dishes, as well as stew and roasted vegetables. We would serve these often for small lunches or dinners. As chefs in the royal kitchens, our culinary mantra was that the food should taste wonderful, look beautiful, be of superior quality, and put guests at ease.

STATE VISITS AND STATE BANQUETS

There are a number of special events that happen each year at Buckingham Palace. The most complex events are state visits and the largest event (besides garden parties) is the annual diplomatic reception.

Medals presented to me by visiting heads of government at state banquets

State banquet menus

Petit fours pastillage on gilt plates ready for the state banquet

The goal of state visits is to help further political or economic solutions between Great Britain and other countries, as well as to cement relationships with longtime allies. They are an important political function of the monarchy and are executed with an eye to modern comfort and a serving of royal style. When the President of the United States makes a royal visit to Britain, he and his entourage are met by the Queen and are transported by royal carriage through the streets of London to Buckingham Palace.

At the palace the guests attend an arrival lunch that usually serves fifty to sixty people. That evening, a formal banquet is held and the guest list expands to include dignitaries and businesspeople. The dinners are served in an enormous ballroom with opulent silver or gold place settings and the meal typically includes five or six courses. When the tables are completely set up, the ballroom is a regal sight, perfectly appropriate for a queen's dinner.

For state banquets, a chef really earns his stripes. Menus are carefully chosen, provisions sent back if they don't meet the highest standards, and sauces are tasted and retasted. The garnishes alone are elaborate and time-consuming. For example, the banquet tables, when fully set, include large fruit baskets. "Basket" is a bit of a misnomer, since they are all highly decorated Meissen china, some footed and some not. Fruit has to be carefully picked, polished, and gently laid on the china. Even the fruit leaves are individually polished and arranged.

Often we made pastillage dishes. These are a

combination of egg whites, powdered sugar, and cornstarch, which can be modeled into all sorts of shapes. The paste would sometimes be formed into delicate little baskets for petit fours with a spun sugar British flag popped on the side of the basket and a flag from the visiting country on the other. They took an enormous amount of time and care to make. Usually I could retrieve a number of these after dinner to reuse again in the future. I say usually, because that was never true when the French visited. After polishing off the petit fours, the French assumed the dish was akin to an ashtray and they would use it to stub out their cigarettes.

On a state visit, each guest would have a silver fruit bowl, a box of chocolates (with the ribbon colors of their country), and some cookies placed in their room. The more important they were, the bigger the fruit bowl and chocolates. The ones for the President's suite are far left.

State banquets did have their perks. After each banquet, the Queen would send each member of the staff two miniature bottles of whiskey or gin. It was her way of saying thank you. Mind you, she was wise to send the bottles *after* the event. Given how stressful state banquets were, it would have been too tempting had we received the bottles beforehand.

Visiting heads of state often gave gifts as well. The most generous visitors? Without a doubt, Arab heads of state. In truth, they also made us work harder. They brought their own chefs to provide halal meals, they often asked for meals at all

A sultan's gift to the Queen, valued at over $500,000. The dessert dish had a marble bowl set on three gilded horses and was decorated with diamonds, rubies, sapphires, and emeralds.

hours, and we had to make certain that specific foods were banned from their chefs' workspace. But they were very generous. Staff was picked to receive watches and brooches, footmen were tipped thousands of pounds for their work, and the kitchen would often get a box of saffron and mangoes from the visiting chef.

The Diplomatic Reception

Another annual event at Buckingham Palace is the diplomatic reception. Each year the Queen hosts one such reception as a way to bring together diplomats and staff from every embassy in London. As many as fifteen hundred people typically attend, and each guest is greeted by the Queen. Now, imagine you are the Queen and you have to say hello to fifteen hundred people before having a strong gin and dubonnet. It's a real workout, believe me.

Royal Politesse

Other members of the royal family often join the Queen during diplomatic receptions. Prince Philip and Prince Charles are usually in attendance, and Princess Diana often came as well. Even after the separation, Princess Diana would attend certain Buckingham Palace functions. She didn't love it, but she was a good trouper all the same. Once, a Saudi Prince cornered her, extolling the virtues of different fruit in his country, especially mangoes. Diana, at a loss for words, told him that indeed she loved mangoes. A week later she lugged a box of mangoes into the kitchen and plopped them down in front of me.

"Do you believe this, Darren?" she said. "That man sent me a whole crate of mangoes because I mentioned that I like them. Next time I need to mention how much I like diamonds."

The chefs get a workout too. Crafting individual canapés for fifteen hundred is mind-boggling. Assuming six hors d'oeuvres per invited guest, we would make about ten thousand canapés. Typically the hot canapés are much more popular than the cold ones. I remember chucking mounds of cold tomato aspic canapés directly into the garbage one year. The use of aspic is a holdover from the Victorian era when jellies could be used to preserve food without requiring refrigeration. But modern dignitaries are used to modern food, and they would devour Stilton and Pecan Sable with Poached Pear or Croques Monsieurs while lobster tails preserved in aspic were returned to the kitchen uneaten.

Teatime and Garden Tea Parties

The Queen is especially fond of teatime. If I was making tea for the Queen and Prince Philip, which was quite often, generally there would be two different types of sandwiches with different fillings. The bread was either whole wheat or white, sliced very thinly and cut into squares with the corners trimmed to create a kind of octagon. I remember early on in my career I asked a fellow chef why it was necessary to trim corners off of tea sandwiches. I was told to never cut a square or a rectangle. It looked too much like a coffin and it meant you wished the Queen ill. I was mindful never to make that mistake.

There were also scones, one large cake, and one small cake such as a fruit tart or éclair. The fillings might vary a bit or the fruit used would change from season to season, but essentially the tea menu was the same every day.

Everyone has a favorite cake and the Queen of England is no exception. Hers is chocolate cake, either with a sponge or biscuit base. Once a chocolate cake is made, the Queen has it brought out again and again at teatime until it is gone. I have even packed half a cake into "Ascot boxes" and sent it along with other provisions to Windsor Castle for the Queen's teas during the weekend.

The Queen requests chocolate sponge cake each year for her birthday. It is basically a dark bittersweet chocolate genoise cut into three layers and each layer filled with a rich chocolate ganache. And I mean rich. The ganache is made with cream from the Windsor dairies. To complete the cake, more hot ganache is poured over the top and allowed to run down the sides. It is excessive and utterly delicious. Any leftover ganache is cooled and used to decorate the cake with a simple "Happy Birthday."

Even more delicious, in my opinion, is the chocolate biscuit cake. All the chefs loved it. One night a fairly new chef must have thought it was *his* birthday when a chocolate biscuit cake was returned from teatime with only a tiny wedge missing. Well, he decided to skip dinner and instead ate his way through the cake, piece by piece, until it was finished. The next day, the head of

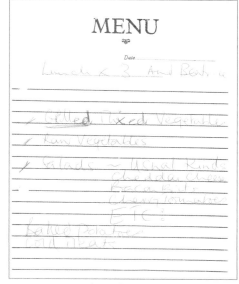

Instructions from the Duchess of York's menu book

The menu of the wedding breakfast for Prince Andrew and Sarah Ferguson, the Duchess of York

pastry was frantically looking for the cake, questioning everyone until finally the sheepish glutton admitted his guilt. We quickly made a new cake and just before it left the kitchen, I cut out a tiny wedge. I am not sure if the Queen ever noticed the substitution.

Of course the Queen was not the only person who liked teatime. Most members of the royal family liked a good afternoon tea. Her Royal Highness the Duchess of York, Sarah Ferguson, loved elaborate afternoon teas. She had an office in Buckingham Palace and regularly held teas for twelve or more. In addition to the regular tea provisions, she would add several more cakes and sausage rolls. She loved Battenburg Cake and I once sent up an absolutely perfect Battenburg Cake that I had made for her tea. It was returned uneaten with instructions not to serve her "store-bought" tea cakes again. A bit of a backhanded compliment I suppose! Oh well, the chefs enjoyed it.

Garden Tea Parties

Garden parties have been hosted by the English monarchy since the late-1800s. The Queen throws four garden parties a year, all but one at Buckingham

Palace. The first party takes place in mid-July. Annual attendance at all the garden events combined typically exceeds thirty thousand people. Invitations are sent out by the Lord Chamberlain's office to government groups, charities, and diplomatic organizations. Dress is important: men are expected to wear morning cutaways, evening suits, or military uniforms, and ladies wear dresses and hats. You can also wear a national costume, like a Scottish kilt. The parties are a

Christmas Ball

Of all my favorite events at Buckingham Palace, I loved the staff Christmas Ball the best. And not just because it meant I didn't have to cook! You were allowed to attend every other year and could bring one member of your family. Over the years, I squired my mom, grandmother, sister, my wife, Wendy, and on one memorable occasion, my father.

I guess it could be seen as a bit singular to take your dad to a ball. But my father was keen to meet Princess Diana and by then she and I had a quite proper but sweet friendship. In fact, I had boasted to my dad that the princess knew me quite well. She had the last laugh though. When she met my dad she pretended to have no idea who I was. My father looked at me in consternation. Laughing it off, Diana asked me to dance and asked my father to hold her purse. Off we went to dance and my father stood there, purse in hand, enchanted.

The Master of the Household
has received Her Majesty's command to invite

Mr Damen McGrady

to a Dance to be given at Buckingham Palace
by The Queen and The Duke of Edinburgh
on Tuesday, 19th December, 1995 at 8.30 p.m.

This card does not admit

Dress: Dinner Jacket
or
Lounge Suit

genuine "thank you" from the Queen to charitable organizations that work so hard throughout the year. Garden parties are extremely popular and provide ordinary Britons a chance to feel like a royal, if only for a few hours!

Central London seems to go back in time on garden party days. The gold and black palace gates swing open at three o'clock to allow all of these quite formally dressed guests to enter—through the first arch, across the quadrangle, into the palace, and out onto the manicured lawns of the Queen's backyard. There is just enough time to get a table, grab a cup or two of Earl Grey tea and a bit of sandwich or cake, before getting a good place in line as the clock strikes four. Then Her Majesty and other royals make their way to the garden steps and the military band plays the national anthem.

The Queen and the junior royals head for the royal tea tent in the far right-hand corner of the garden; they all take a different route in order to shake hands with their guests. By the time the Queen reaches the royal tent she is grateful for a pot of Earl Grey and a scoop of homemade ice cream. If Her Majesty is especially hungry, she can choose from a variety of sandwiches and fillings, large slices of cake, jam tarts or fruit tarts, éclairs, ice cream, four different kinds of cakes including scones, and iced coffee. The large cakes might vary, but usually include a sponge cake with cream filling, a chocolate cake, a lemon cake, or a ginger cake.

CROQUES MONSIEUR

This is a traditional appetizer that we probably made for just about every reception. Everyone loved them, which is no surprise. After all, they are layers of smoked ham and Gruyère cheese sandwiched between heavily buttered bread and then broiled. What is not to like?

1 stick salted butter, softened

8 slices *pain de mie* or firm white bread

8 ounces Gruyère cheese, 16 thin slices with rind removed

8 (1-ounce) slices smoked ham

1. Preheat the broiler. Butter the bread slices on both sides. Top 4 slices of bread with 8 thin slices of Gruyère, followed by all 8 slices of ham. Finish with the remaining Gruyère on top of the ham, and then lay the remaining 4 bread slices on top of the cheese.

2. Put the croques monsieur onto a baking sheet, and place the baking sheet under the broiler for 5 to 8 minutes, or until the bread turns golden brown and crispy. Flip the sandwiches over carefully, and brown the other side. Remove the four sandwiches from the broiler, trim off the crusts, and cut each sandwich into eight pieces. Serve immediately.

3. If you plan to make the croques monsieur ahead of time, they can be laid between layers of parchment paper and refrigerated.

MAKES 32 COCKTAIL-SIZE PORTIONS

GLENEAGLES PÂTÉ

This was a popular first course at Buckingham Palace and a favorite of the Queen's for private meals. It is a combination of three pâtés: smoked salmon, smoked trout, and smoked mackerel, which are layered on smoked salmon fillets and sliced. Served with Melba toast and horseradish crème fraîche, a small portion goes a long way in flavor. It keeps well and can be multiplied to serve a crowd.

2   pounds smoked salmon, thinly sliced and divided

1   pound smoked trout

6   sticks (1½ pounds) unsalted butter, softened and divided

1   tablespoon finely chopped fresh dill

1   teaspoon lemon juice

1   pound smoked mackerel

1   tablespoon finely chopped fresh chives

1. Line a 1-pound loaf tin or pâté terrine with plastic wrap, overlapping the sides. Take half of the smoked salmon and line the sides and bottom of the loaf tin. Overlap the top edge by about 2 inches so that the salmon will fold over and cover the filling once it is in place.

2. Remove and discard the skin from the smoked trout, and then place the trout in a food processor and chop finely; add 2 sticks (½ pound) of the butter to the processor. Blend again until smooth and add the chopped dill and lemon juice. Carefully spread the trout mixture into the loaf tin on top of the smoked salmon and smooth the top. Place the loaf tin in the freezer for 10 minutes while you prepare the second layer.

3. Clean the food processor bowl. Remove and discard the skin from the mackerel, and place the mackerel into the food processor; chop finely. Add 2 sticks butter and blend until smooth. Take the loaf tin from the freezer, and spread the mackerel mixture smoothly on top of the trout layer without disturbing the trout layer. Place the loaf tin in the freezer for 10 minutes while you prepare the third layer.

4. Clean the food processor bowl once again and place the remaining smoked salmon into the food processor and chop finely. Add the remaining 2 sticks of butter and the chives to the processor, and blend again until smooth. Remove the loaf tin from the freezer, and spread the smoked salmon on top of the mackerel. Smooth the top.

5. Fold the overlapping pieces of smoked salmon over the top layer of the salmon spread. Cover the top with plastic wrap, and refrigerate overnight, or for at least 4 hours, until firm.

6. Remove the loaf tin from the refrigerator, and lift off the top plastic wrap. Invert the terrine onto a cutting board and remove the loaf tin and additional plastic wrap. Slice the terrine into 1-inch slices. Serve on salad leaves as an appetizer or slice the terrine into fingers and serve on crackers as a canapé.

MAKES 8 TO 10 SERVINGS

CHILLED TOMATO AND DILL MOUSSE WITH LOBSTER

This delicate, subtle tomato mousse was often served at state banquets. It became a favorite of Princess Diana's, but she wasn't keen on the sour cream, heavy cream, and mayonnaise that make it so rich. So I devised a fat-free version of the same dish for her. The princess would have the mousse along with poached lobster. Her guests would receive the full-fat version and everyone was happy. (The recipe for the fat-free version appears on page 199.)

1/2	teaspoon vegetable oil	1	small bunch fresh dill, finely chopped
1	pound ripe tomatoes, chopped	1 1/2	packets unflavored gelatin
3	tablespoons finely minced onion	1	lemon, halved
1/2	cup mayonnaise	6	(7-ounce) lobster tails, steamed and split down the center
1/2	cup sour cream		
1/4	cup heavy cream	1/4	cup extra-virgin olive oil
1	tablespoon tomato paste	1	bunch fresh chives, chopped
	Salt and freshly ground pepper	3	bunches watercress, washed and stems removed

1. Lightly brush six small ramekins with the vegetable oil and set aside.

2. In a food processor, puree the tomatoes with the chopped onion. Strain the pulp into a bowl, pressing on the tomatoes to push as much as possible through the sieve into the bowl. In a separate bowl, combine the mayonnaise, sour cream, heavy cream, and tomato paste. Fold into the tomato/onion puree. Add a pinch of salt and pepper and the finely chopped dill. Stir to combine.

3. Place the gelatin into a small saucepan, and moisten it with the juice of 1/2 of the lemon. If the lemon doesn't have a lot of juice, you may need to add up to a tablespoon of water. Reserve the remaining 1/2 lemon for the lobster vinaigrette. Melt the gelatin over a very low heat until it dissolves. Let it cool a moment, and then pour the gelatin into the tomato mousse, mixing as you pour. Taste for salt and pepper.

4. Pour the finished mixture into the ramekins and refrigerate for at least 1 hour. Just before serving, run a small knife around the edge of the mold, dip the ramekin into a bowl of hot water to soften the gelatin, and turn out the mousse onto a plate.

5. Toss the split lobster tails with the olive oil, remaining lemon juice, salt, pepper, and chopped chives. Nestle the lobster on a bed of watercress right next to the tomato mousse.

MAKES 6 SERVINGS

STILTON AND PECAN SABLÉS WITH GRILLED PEARS

This makes a delicate canapé, rich in flavor. The buttery, nutty, sandy base disintegrates in your mouth, leaving a smooth combination of blue cheese and soft pear.

6	ounces chopped pecans	1	pound Stilton cheese, crumbled
3	cups flour	1	ripe pear
1/2	teaspoon celery seeds	1	teaspoon walnut oil
1/4	teaspoon cayenne pepper	8	ounces goat cheese, softened
2	sticks (1 cup) unsalted butter, at room temperature	1	bunch fresh dill

1. Preheat the oven to 350 degrees. Roast the pecans in the oven on a baking sheet for about 15 minutes. Cool and finely chop the nuts. In a separate large bowl, mix together the flour, celery seeds, and cayenne pepper. Cut in the softened butter, continuing until the flour mixture has the consistency of bread crumbs. Add the cheese, and mix well into the flour mixture; then add the pecans. Collect the dough into a ball, and place it on a sheet of parchment paper. Use the parchment paper to roll the dough into a log about 1 inch thick. Chill in the refrigerator until the dough is firm.

2. Cut the chilled dough into 1/4-inch round slices, and place the slices 2 inches apart on a baking sheet lined with parchment paper. Cook for 15 minutes, or until the sablés just start to color. Remove from the oven, lift onto a cooling rack, and allow to cool completely. The sablés can then be kept in an airtight container for several days.

3. When ready to serve, first quarter and peel the pear, removing the core and tossing the pear quarters in the walnut oil. Either broil or grill the pear quarters until they begin to soften. Remove from the oven or grill, and allow them to cool. While the pears are cooling, place the softened goat cheese in a piping bag fitted with a small star tube, and pipe a rosette of goat cheese on each sablé. Decorate each with a thin slice of the grilled pear, and top each pear slice with a tiny sprig of dill.

MAKES 50 PIECES

HERBED CREPES WITH GOAT CHEESE AND MAPLE SALMON

Crepes

1¹/2 cups flour
¹/4 teaspoon salt
1 egg
2 egg yolks
2¹/2 cups milk
¹/2 cup fresh chopped herbs including dill, tarragon, chives, parsley
Freshly ground pepper
¹/2 stick (¹/4 cup) unsalted butter
1 tablespoon vegetable oil

Filling

1¹/2 pounds center-cut Atlantic salmon, skinned
¹/2 cup Grade A maple syrup
¹/2 cup Dijon mustard
2 cups softened goat cheese
1 small bunch fresh dill

1. Preheat the oven to 400 degrees.

2. **For the crepes,** whisk together the flour and salt in a large bowl. Add the egg and egg yolks followed by the milk, herbs, and black pepper. Continue whisking until there are no visible lumps. Melt the butter in a small pan over medium heat until it is golden brown. Whisk the butter into the crepes mixture and let the batter rest for about 15 minutes.

3. Heat an 8-inch crepe pan or small frying pan. Add the vegetable oil and spread it around the base of the pan. Carefully heat the oil until it starts to smoke, then pour the oil into a small bowl for later use if needed. Return the pan to the heat.

4. Pour about 2 tablespoons of the batter into the crepe pan, tilting the pan to coat the base evenly. Cook until the base is golden brown, and then turn or toss to cook the other side. Turn out the crepe onto a large dinner plate, and repeat with the remaining batter, stacking the crepes on top of each other. Let cool.

5. **For the filling,** place the salmon on a small baking sheet, and pour the maple syrup over the salmon. Bake in the top part of the oven for 5 minutes, remove from the oven, and spoon any syrup left on the tray back onto the salmon. Bake for an additional 8 minutes. Remove from the oven, again spoon the syrup on the tray over the salmon, and allow the salmon to cool. Flake the salmon into small, bite-size pieces, and reserve.

Reception canapés: Herbed Crepes with Goat Cheese and Maple Salmon, Sausage Rolls, Stilton and Pecan Sablés with Grilled Pears, Croques Monsieur

6. Lay out the crepes, several at a time, with the browner side facing up. Trim the edges of the crepes to make squares. Spread each square with a fine layer of Dijon mustard. Crumble a bit of the goat cheese along the bottom inch of each crepe. Then spread some of the salmon on top of the goat cheese. Roll the crepes up as you would a jelly roll, and refrigerate for about 30 minutes. Remove from the refrigerator, and cut into 1-inch pieces on a slant. Lay the crepes on their sides so you can see the filling, and garnish each piece with a sprig of fresh dill.

MAKES APPROXIMATELY 48 APPETIZERS

SAUSAGE ROLLS

1½ pounds good quality pork sausage
1   teaspoon dried basil
1   teaspoon dried oregano
1   teaspoon dried thyme

Salt and freshly ground pepper
1   (17-ounce) package frozen puff pastry, thawed
2   eggs, beaten

1. Preheat the oven to 375 degrees. In a large bowl mix together the sausage, basil, oregano, thyme, and salt and pepper to taste until all the seasonings are well distributed throughout.

2. Roll out all of the puff pastry into one large rectangle about ⅛ inch thick. Put the wide side of the rectangle to your left. Form the sausage meat into a log about 1 inch thick and long enough to fit the width of the pastry. Lay this log along the wide edge. Roll the pastry around the sausage, brush with beaten eggs at the join, and cut so that the pastry has just enough room to slightly overlap. Repeat the process with the remaining sausage meat and pastry. Line up all of the sausage rolls making sure the seam on each is at the bottom and not showing. Brush the tops with the eggs and cut the sausage rolls into either 1½- or 3-inch logs.

3. Spread about one inch apart on a baking sheet, and bake until golden brown and the meat is cooked, about 15 to 20 minutes. You can also freeze the rolls to be cooked later. Serve warm or cold.

MAKES 24 3-INCH ROLLS
OR 48 1½-INCH APPETIZER ROLLS

GAELIC STEAKS

When Gaelic is in the title, be prepared for whiskey in the ingredients. This recipe is no exception. It's a hands-down favorite of the Duke of Edinburgh's, who would have it on the menu every day if he had his way. The sauce is a quick pan sauce of mushrooms, shallots, parsley, whiskey, and cream. It is an impressive meal for private dinners and yet easy enough for the Duke to make on his own to impress guests at summer barbeques.

I add Marmite to this dish to give it some depth and richness. Marmite is a dark brown colored yeast extract made in the UK. It is rich in vitamin B and has a strong, unique, slightly salty flavor. Don't season your sauce until after you have reduced it and added the Marmite.

1 1/2 pounds beef tenderloin, cut into 4 equal steaks	1 cup heavy cream
Salt and freshly ground pepper	1/2 chicken bouillon cube, dissolved in 1 cup boiling water *or* 1 cup homemade chicken broth
4 tablespoons olive oil, divided	1/4 teaspoon Marmite
1 large onion, finely chopped	2 tablespoons whiskey
1 clove garlic, chopped	1 tablespoon finely chopped fresh parsley
3 ounces Baby Bella Mushrooms, washed and sliced	

1. Let the steaks come to room temperature and season with salt and pepper to taste. In a sauté pan large enough to fit all the steaks in one layer, add 2 tablespoons olive oil, and heat the pan until hot, but not smoking. Add the steaks and cook each side to medium rare, about 4 to 6 minutes. Remove the steaks to a warm plate and cover.

2. In the same pan, add the remaining 2 tablespoons olive oil, and warm the oil over a medium flame. Add the onion and sauté until translucent. Stir in the garlic and mushrooms, and sauté until the mushrooms soften and lose some of their moisture. Add the cream, bouillon or broth, Marmite, and whiskey. Increase the heat to high, and reduce the liquid until it forms a sauce thick enough to coat the back of a wooden spoon.

3. Remove the sauce from the heat, and check the seasoning. Add to the sauce any accumulated juices from the steaks. Place each steak on a plate, spoon the sauce on top, and garnish with the chopped parsley.

MAKES 4 SERVINGS

SPINACH SOUFFLÉ

This spinach soufflé was usually served as a vegetable side dish, but sometimes it was served as dessert. Her Majesty would write "savoury" in the menu book and this meant that she wanted to end her meal with something like a savory soufflé. It would be served piping hot with a jug of Windsor cream alongside to drizzle into the center.

When we made spinach soufflés as a vegetable, the presentation was quite classic. We spooned the mixture into eight-inch ring molds, and while they were baking we sautéed wild mushrooms in a cream sauce. The finished soufflés would be inverted onto a silver dish, the ring mold removed, and the mushrooms spooned into the center. A sprinkle of chopped tarragon was placed on top and off to the table they went.

Softened butter for greasing	1 1/4 cups milk
1 (20-ounce) bag spinach, or enough to make 1 cup spinach puree	1/2 cup heavy cream
1/2 cup all-purpose flour	4 eggs, separated
4 tablespoons unsalted butter	1/2 teaspoon freshly grated nutmeg
	Salt and freshly ground pepper

1. Preheat the oven to 400 degrees. Liberally butter an 8-inch soufflé dish, leaving a 1/8-inch thick ring of butter around the lip.

2. Drop the spinach into a large pan of boiling water for 30 seconds, and then strain into a colander. Refresh the spinach by placing it back into the empty saucepan and filling the pan with cold water. Once the spinach is cold, strain it again and drain off as much water as possible. Squeeze the spinach in a clean tea towel to remove the excess water, and then puree it in a food processor. You will need to reserve 1 cup of the puree for the soufflé. Any extra spinach can be blended with mayonnaise, garlic, and red wine vinegar to make a sauce verte.

3. In a heavy saucepan, add the flour, butter, milk, and cream, and whisk together over high heat until the butter melts and a thick sauce forms. Remove from the heat, and whisk in the egg yolks, nutmeg, and the spinach. Season with the salt and pepper to taste, and allow to cool for about 10 minutes.

4. Whisk the egg whites until stiff, and fold into the spinach mix until all white egg traces have disappeared. Pour into the soufflé dish, and place it on the middle shelf in

the oven. Bake for 20 minutes, or until the soufflé rises and is slightly firm to the touch on the top.

5. Remove from the oven and serve immediately with a jug of heavy cream.

MAKES 6 SERVINGS

SAGE DERBY DAUPHINOISE POTATOES

Sage Derby cheese is an old British cheese dating from the 1700s. It was made only once a year and was consumed for medicinal purposes because the fresh sage added to the cheese curds was reputed to have curative powers. Over time, the green-colored cheese became popular at Christmas, in keeping with the decorated wreaths and trees. It remains a popular Christmas treat, but is good any time of the year. Many reputable cheese shops carry it, but in a pinch, Gruyère makes a fine substitute.

2½ cups heavy cream, divided	1 cup grated Parmesan cheese
5 pounds large redskin potatoes, peeled and very thinly sliced	4 cloves garlic, crushed
8 ounces (about 2 cups) Sage Derby cheese or Gruyère, grated	Salt and freshly ground pepper

1. Preheat the oven to 400 degrees. Pour ½ cup heavy cream on the bottom of a 13 x 9-inch, oval casserole. Place a layer of sliced potatoes on top of the cream. The potatoes should be about ¼ inch thick, and although you can slice them by hand, I find a mandolin does a great job as well. Over the first layer of potatoes, sprinkle some of the Sage Derby and Parmesan cheese, followed by some of the garlic and a dusting of salt and pepper and another ½ cup of cream. Continue building layers (you'll have about three), finishing with the cheese and the remaining cream.

2. Cover the casserole dish with aluminum foil and bake in the center of the oven for about 45 minutes. Remove the aluminum foil and bake for another 30 minutes, or until the potatoes are tender and the top is golden brown.

3. Remove from the oven and serve immediately, or allow to cool overnight in the refrigerator. The dauphinoise can be reheated gently in the oven as a whole, or you can cut out shapes with a cookie cutter and reheat on a baking sheet.

MAKES 8 SERVINGS

RASPBERRY ICE CREAM

This recipe makes an intensely flavored raspberry ice cream that is delicious on its own and even better when spooned into brandy snap cornets (recipe page 69) and topped with a dollop of clotted cream.

4	cups fresh raspberries
1	cup plus 2 tablespoons sugar
1¼	cups heavy cream
½	cup milk
2	lemons, juiced

1. Puree the raspberries in a blender and pour into a large bowl. Add the sugar, cream, milk, and lemon juice, and whisk together. Strain the mix through a fine sieve to remove the seeds.

2. Pour into an ice cream maker to freeze, following manufacturer's instructions. If you don't have an ice cream machine, you can still make this dish. Instead of pouring the cream into the raspberry puree, whip it until stiff instead and fold it into the mix. Freeze in a plastic container for about 3 hours, remove from the freezer, and stir. Repeat this process several times, and then freeze until firm.

MAKES 6 SERVINGS

Garden party fare: (from left to right) Chocolate Biscuit Cake, Jam and Cream Sponge, Battenburg Cake, tea sandwiches, Raspberry Ice Cream

BATTENBURG CAKE

Battenburg Cake is a traditional English tea cake, despite its German name. The Battenburg family went on to become the Mountbatten family, changing their name to Windsor just before World War I. This cake is still served at Buckingham Palace, especially for garden parties, and was a favorite of the Duchess of York's.

4	sticks (1 pound) unsalted butter, softened	3	to 4 drops red food color (optional)
2¼	cups granulated sugar	1	(12-ounce) jar apricot jam
8	eggs	1	pound marzipan
3¼	cups all-purpose flour	1	tablespoon powdered sugar

1. Preheat the oven to 350 degrees. Grease two 9-inch cake pans, and line with greased parchment paper. In a mixing bowl, cream the butter and sugar until pale, light, and fluffy. Gradually beat in the eggs one at a time. Fold in the flour, and place half of the mixture into one of the prepared cake tins. Quickly fold in a few drops of the red food color (any more will make it a darker red) into the remaining cake batter until well combined, and then pour the red batter into the other prepared cake pan.

2. Bake for 30 minutes, or until golden brown and the top of each cake springs back when lightly pressed. Remove from the oven, and invert the cake pans onto a cooling rack. Leave to cool completely.

3. Trim each cake into two 7 x 1 x 1-inch rectangles, four in all. Try to remove all the brown outer edges when you are cutting the rectangular logs. In a small pan, melt the apricot jam over low heat to soften. Brush jam onto all the sides of each of the four pieces. Lay a plain layer of cake with a red layer on top. Touching alongside the plain layer, lay a red layer with a plain layer on top.

4. Roll out the marzipan to about ¼ inch thick and into a rectangle big enough to wrap around the cake. Carefully lay the cake on one edge of the marzipan, and fold the marzipan around the cake, moistening the marzipan edges with a little water and pinching them together. Trim off any marzipan edges and discard. Cut the cake into 1-inch slices and serve.

MAKES 10 SERVINGS

CHOCOLATE BISCUIT CAKE

OK, you have to first understand that when I say "biscuit," I am referring to "cookies," not those big muffin-looking things you eat at breakfast to keep the bacon grease off your hands! In Britain, biscuits are cookies . . . and cookies . . . well those are things that keep popping up on your computer screens. That explained, this is an amazing no-bake cake best served straight from the refrigerator. I can't say how long it keeps because I have never had one last longer than five minutes before I was staring at a plate of crumbs.

Without a doubt, it is the Queen's favorite tea cake. We had request after request from palace visitors to divulge the recipe. Well, I've held out until now. Enjoy!

1/2 teaspoon butter, for greasing pan	4 ounces dark chocolate
8 ounces McVities rich tea biscuits	1 egg, beaten
1/2 stick (4 tablespoons) unsalted butter, softened	8 ounces dark chocolate, for icing
1/2 cup granulated sugar	1 ounce white chocolate, for decoration

1. Lightly grease a small (such as 6 x 2 1/2-inch) cake ring with 1/2 teaspoon butter, and place on a parchment-lined tray. Break each of the biscuits into almond-size pieces by hand and set aside. Cream the butter and sugar in a bowl until the mixture is a light lemon color.

2. Melt the 4 ounces of dark chocolate in a double boiler. Add the butter and sugar mixture to the chocolate, stirring constantly. Add the egg and continue stirring. Fold in the biscuit pieces until they are all coated with the chocolate mixture.

3. Spoon the chocolate biscuit mixture into the prepared cake ring. Try to fill all of the gaps on the bottom of the ring, because this will be the top when it is unmolded. Chill the cake in the refrigerator for at least three hours.

4. Remove the cake from the refrigerator, and let it stand while you melt the 8 ounces of dark chocolate for icing. Slide the ring off the cake and turn the cake upside down onto a cooling rack. Pour the 8 ounces of melted dark chocolate over the cake, and smooth the top and sides using a butter knife or offset spatula. Allow the chocolate icing to set at room temperature. Carefully run a knife around the bottom of the cake where it has stuck to the cooling rack, and transfer the cake to a cake dish. Melt the white chocolate and drizzle on top of the cake in a decorative pattern.

MAKES 8 SERVINGS

EARL GREY TEA CAKE

Earl Grey is the most often served tea at Buckingham Palace. It is a black tea flavored with oil of Bergamot—a fragrant citrus fruit—and named after the second Earl Grey in 1830. Needless to say, it also makes a wonderful scented tea cake that stays moist for weeks.

1¼ cups boiling water	3 eggs
¾ cup Earl Grey loose tea leaves	1½ cups all-purpose flour
1 stick (8 tablespoons) unsalted butter, plus extra for greasing the pan	½ cup ground almonds
1½ cups Demerara or light brown sugar, packed	4 cups raisins
	½ cup walnuts, chopped
	Crème fraîche (optional)

1. Preheat the oven to 350 degrees. Line a loaf pan with parchment paper and grease the parchment with butter. Pour the boiling water over the tea leaves in a large bowl, and leave the mixture to infuse for at least 1 hour. Strain the tea, and set aside to cool.

2. Cream the butter and sugar until light and smooth. Gradually incorporate the eggs, beating well after each addition. Fold in the flour and ground almonds, followed by the raisins and walnuts. Add the reserved tea and mix well.

3. Spoon the batter into the prepared loaf pan, and bake for 1 hour, or until a toothpick inserted into the center comes out clean. Remove the cake from the oven, and cool in the pan set on a cooling rack. When it is cool, unmold the cake, slice, and serve topped with crème fraîche. Any leftover cake can be wrapped in plastic wrap and refrigerated for up to several weeks.

MAKES 12 SERVINGS

JAM AND CREAM SWISS ROLL

1	tablespoon unsalted butter, softened	1¼	cups potato flour or potato starch
2	tablespoons all-purpose flour	1	(12-ounce) jar strawberry jelly or jam
8	eggs, separated	1	pint (2 cups) heavy cream, whipped to soft peaks
1½	cups granulated sugar plus ½ cup for sprinkling		

1. Preheat the oven to 350 degrees. Line a 13 x 9-inch baking sheet with parchment paper. Lightly grease the paper with the butter, and then dust with the flour. Whisk the egg yolks and 1½ cups sugar with an electric mixer or beater on high until the mixture turns pale in color, about 3 minutes. Whisk the egg whites with an electric mixer or beater on high until soft peaks form.

2. Fold half the egg whites into the yolk and sugar mixture, followed by the potato flour, and then the remaining half of the egg whites. Gently pour the mixture into the prepared pan and smooth out to the corners with an offset spatula. Bake for 10 to 15 minutes in the center of the oven. Check to see if the sponge cake is cooked by gently pressing the top; it will spring back when done. Have ready a sheet of parchment paper (at least 13 x 9-inches) sprinkled with the remaining ½ cup granulated sugar. Turn the sponge cake out onto the sugared parchment paper and peel off the baking parchment. Allow the cake to cool. Spread the cake lightly with the jam and whipped cream. Roll the cake into a tight spiral, using the parchment paper so not to touch the cake. Slice and serve.

MAKES 8 SERVINGS

RASPBERRY TARTLETS

These always seemed to be on the menu for large garden parties at Buckingham Palace. It took forever to place three raspberries of the same size on each tartlet and then to "paint" each one with raspberry jam. Sometimes we would put half a strawberry on the tartlets brushed with raspberry jam, or mandarin orange segments, brushed with apricot jam. Any leftover pastry can be kept in the refrigerator for at least four weeks.

Pastry

1	cup sugar
1	stick ($\frac{1}{2}$ cup) plus 6 tablespoons unsalted butter
1	teaspoon vanilla paste
1	egg
$3\frac{1}{4}$	cups all-purpose flour

Filling

$1\frac{3}{4}$	cups milk
$\frac{1}{4}$	cup heavy cream
2	whole eggs
4	egg yolks
$\frac{1}{4}$	cup cornstarch
2	teaspoons vanilla paste
$\frac{3}{4}$	cup sugar
	Pinch of salt
3	cups fresh raspberries
1	(12-ounce) jar seedless raspberry jam

1. **For the pastry,** cream the sugar, butter, and vanilla paste in a mixing bowl until pale. Beat in the egg until combined. Fold in the flour, form the dough into a ball, and refrigerate for at least 1 hour.

2. **For the filling,** bring the milk and cream to a boil in a small heavy saucepan over a high heat. Place the whole eggs, egg yolks, cornstarch, vanilla, sugar, and salt in a large bowl, and whisk together. Pour the boiling milk and cream over the egg mixture, and whisk together. Return the mixture to the pan, and whisk over a low heat until the mix starts to thicken. Pour into a small container, and cover with plastic wrap. Refrigerate until cold.

3. Roll out the pastry to about $\frac{1}{8}$ inch thick on a lightly floured surface, and using a round cookie cutter, cut out circles to line 24 (2-inch) tartlet molds. Bake the pastry circles in the center of the oven for 15 minutes or until golden brown. Allow the pastry to cool slightly before removing from the molds to a cooling rack.

4. Spoon 1/2 teaspoon of filling into each tartlet, and arrange three raspberries side by side on top of the filling. Heat the jam in a small saucepan over a low heat, stirring until the jam dissolves. Using a pastry brush, brush each of the raspberries with the jam, allowing a little to run into the tartlet.

MAKES 24 INDIVIDUAL TARTLETS

ICED COFFEE

Iced coffee was made at Buckingham Palace for garden parties and at Windsor Castle for Ascot Races tea. The coffee room maid would bring two gallons of freshly brewed Higgins–blend coffee to the kitchen each day and it would chill overnight. Then Windsor cream and sugar syrup was added. The coffee was then decanted through a muslin cloth into chilled coffee urns.

2	cups water	5	cups very strong freshly ground coffee, brewed and chilled
1	cup sugar	1 1/4	cups heavy cream

Put the water and sugar in a small pan, and bring to a boil over high heat. Reduce by half, and remove from the heat to cool completely. In a large bowl mix the coffee and cream, and stir until combined. Whisk in the sugar syrup. Strain through a fine sieve into a large jug and refrigerate. Pour over a glass of ice cubes to serve.

MAKES 2 QUARTS

CHAPTER THREE

Windsor Castle

Rites of Spring

Windsor Castle, sitting timelessly amid its lush acres of parks, lawns, and ponds, seamlessly links England past with England present. It is a breathtaking piece of country. As you walk the enormous expanse of Great Park and Home Park, you can see white swans circling lazily in the Thames or small deer gathering in copses of ancient bent oaks. Men in traditional whites may be assembling for a serious game of cricket. Look up and you'll see flying above it all the royal standard if the Queen is at home. Everything around you seems to say, "This is England!"

I always enjoyed my time at Windsor immensely. Its beauty and timeworn grace make it much loved by family and staff alike. For me, Windsor Castle is linked with memories of springtime in England. Her Majesty begins her stay right before Easter and the family is at the castle off and on through the spring and into early summer. Many great events take place after Easter, including two of my favorites: the Ascot Races and the Royal Horse Show. Also, lots of wonderful food begins showing up in the spring, including luscious hothouse peaches, fragile and deeply flavored strawberries—I mean real strawberries the likes of which we don't often see anymore—and thick luscious cream culled from the Windsor cows that have been pastured outdoors in the meadows surrounding the castle.

Windsor Ablaze

Windsor Castle is old, even by English standards. It has been a royal residence for almost one thousand years. But nothing stays the same forever, and so Windsor has changed with time. Some changes reflect the desires of previous royalty or the slow wearing effects of nature. And some changes happen from unforeseen disaster. I witnessed one of those disasters, for I was living on the grounds of the castle on November 20, 1992, when a fire broke out in the Queen's private chapel in the northeast part of the castle and rapidly moved to engulf the state apartments.

The castle's part-time twenty-man fire brigade was dispatched along with a local firehouse. The fire quickly spread to the Brunswick Tower and the Royal Berkshire Fire and Rescue Service were called in, plus an additional ten firehouses. Even that proved to be insufficient. By the end of the day thirty-nine firehouses were on-site battling the blaze.

I remember it quite clearly. I had just arrived at Windsor and settled into my apartment at Frogmore Stables. It was midafternoon when I got a knock on the door from one of the gardeners who had been sent to rally the staff to the castle. Word came that a fire had broken out and all hands were required. It wasn't until I was outside and saw all the smoke that I recognized how serious a fire it was. Her Majesty was in the midst of it, directing staff as they gathered up as many irreplaceable treasures as possible. I began helping the firemen, unloading spent oxygen tanks off of firemen's backs and putting on fresh ones so they could go back inside.

At some point the Queen's page, Paul Whybrew, came up and asked me to help clear out the Queen's apartment in the castle. It was the first time I had been inside Her Majesty's apartment. The corridor leading from her rooms to the rest of the castle had been boarded up to help slow the fire's spread; as yet, there wasn't any smoke. Inside, Paul and I started picking up paintings and furniture and carting them out as quickly as we could.

For a time it was just the Queen and me as we packed her personal items. I could see she was terribly distressed though her demeanor was calm. At one point I remember she picked up her husband's slippers and stared at them. I was struck by the thought that all the money and position in the world means nothing at a time like this.

It had been a beautiful clear day and the sun setting over the raging fire was a raw spectacle for our eyes.

Even before nightfall I knew Windsor Castle had been absolutely devastated. It would take five years and millions of pounds to rebuild it.

THE KITCHEN AT WINDSOR CASTLE

There is one main kitchen at Windsor Castle. It's been updated over time—electricity and running water were added more than one hundred years ago—but the original structure remains essentially unchanged and dates back hundreds of years. It is an impressive room to work in—an enormous stone barrel-vaulted room with great distances from sinks to ovens and hearths and to refrigerators. In fact, it takes almost five minutes to walk from the refrigerator to the stoves. Long distances separate the dishwashing area, larder, silver pantry, linen room, and dining room. The farthest is the coffee room. The larder chef has to take tea sandwiches down each afternoon, followed by the pastry chef with scones and tea cakes. Round trip is about twenty minutes. You could have eaten all the food along the way—just to keep up your strength, of course.

Called the Great Kitchen, it is split into three parts. The main kitchen takes care of entrees and vegetables, the larder kitchen prepares all the cold foods, and the royal pastry kitchen is responsible for puddings, pastries, and dessert fruit. The main kitchen, with about a dozen chefs working full time, was a fun place to work when court was in residence. We needed that many chefs. Chefs feed everyone, not just the royal family. At Windsor that includes all staff, stewards, officials and senior officials, butlers, porters, junior chefs, and housemaids. And don't forget the typists, secretaries, and personal assistants.

In an odd twist of bureaucratic space allocation, Windsor Castle has its own fully stocked bar situated right across from the kitchen. With a break between sending up royal meals and getting staff meals out, a senior chef might disappear to the "canteen" for a quick pint . . . and then another. I remember several Windsor weekends when junior chefs cooked the entire dinner because the senior chef was rather tipsy from a convivial visit to the canteen.

At least the kitchens had windows and we could see daylight. The larder kitchen windows look out onto the North Terrace and on quiet days the tourists were fed samples of "royal" food. Goodness knows how many vacation photos have been taken with a gaggle of chefs all posing at the larder window!

The kitchen's workbenches were very old and very low. So low, in fact, that the chefs had wooden blocks made to hold chopping boards eighteen inches off the tables. I'm fairly tall; I always left Windsor with a bad back from bending over those tables while working. The stoves were tucked away in little alcoves and chefs would knock their hats off as they bent to look into a pan. I believe it was the working kitchen most hated by the chefs, but it was the prettiest and had the most character.

Under the larder kitchen was another room that we used as a spare kitchen during busy times. And beneath that was a big empty cave. It was an excellent location for staff discos. I became the resident DJ, spinning old 45 records for the Royal Household Social Club. Dancing would start around ten o'clock, after the staff had finished work, and went on sometimes until after two o'clock in the morning. Of course by then most of the chefs were hungry again.

Lucky for us we had to walk through the kitchen and knew where to find the key to the larder fridge. Many a night we could be found making Scooby-snack–sized sandwiches to eat in the Brunswick Tower elevator before retiring to bed. The next morning we would all tiptoe around the breakfast chef who would be cursing us under his breath as he quickly defrosted bread for the royal breakfast.

WINDSOR WEEKEND

"Windsor weekends" is the name given to the time the Queen spends at Windsor when she is actually in residence at Buckingham Palace. When she heads up to Windsor Castle, the Buckingham Palace kitchen sends lots of food along in two large Ascot boxes, one with food from the main kitchen and another filled with provisions from the pastry kitchen. As senior pastry chef it was my job on Friday to make sure that everything was set to go into the van.

Did the Queen want apple pie? OK, the sweet pastry was packed and I double-checked that the Granny Smith apples were on the fruit order. Chocolate mousse? I added a block of D6 dark chocolate to the box. Coffee mousse? Was there a jar of Nestle Gold Blend and some liqueur coffee beans in there? Check. Beef Wellington? Don't forget the puff pastry. Brandy snaps for tea? I'll just pop in a recipe and the wooden dowels to mold them. Pain Pruneaux? I needed to send the Victorian copper mold to make it in and more importantly, make sure the mold was returned on Monday. Scones and Friday afternoon tea cakes and tea sandwiches were a must and were added alongside the rest of the weekend's ingredients. I tried not to forget anything, but occasionally there was a lapse and over the telephone I had to calm panicked chefs looking for a missing ingredient.

Provisioning the Kitchen

The greatest asset for drivers who deliver food to Windsor Castle is a mild temperament. After a congested twenty-mile drive from London, deliverymen have to haul boxes of food down a flight of stairs, along the basement corridor, and up another flight of stairs to the kitchen. It's not so bad if the Queen hasn't arrived at the castle yet. Then the trucks are allowed into the quadrangle and closer to the staff dining-room-door entrance to unload. But if the Queen is in residence, no trucks are allowed in the yard and provisions have to be carried in from even farther away.

Some of the foods that made their way to the kitchen were gifts received by the Queen. I remember one such gift, a delivery of ripe mangoes from a Saudi prince. On this occasion we had instructions that the fruit was for the Queen and Duke only. Prince Andrew had stopped in the kitchen, seen the mangoes, and asked for one. Robert Pine, the Queen's pastry chef of thirty years, flatly told him, "No. They are for the Queen only."

I put my head down and carried on rolling out pastry. Had a chef just told a member of the royal family no? Prince Andrew was clever, though, and he came back to the kitchen when he knew all the chefs would be at breakfast. Chef Pine was cleverer yet. He had locked the door to the fruit room. For the Queen and the Duke only—those were the orders.

Windsor weekends meant just a few chefs were needed. Typically there was a senior cook in charge and two junior cooks. Not many of the royal family were about, either. Most often it was just the Queen for meals, or perhaps the Queen and the Duke. I loved that because it meant I got to cook everything on the menu, not just sauces or desserts, like the more regimented partie system in place at Buckingham Palace. No, as a senior chef at Windsor Castle I was responsible for it all and that was fine with me. Not so for some other chefs.

I remember one senior chef who hated making dessert. He just couldn't do it. So, one weekend he had a junior chef prepare a chocolate soufflé for the royal dinner. The poor young chef was so nervous—especially when he opened the oven and realized the soufflé hadn't risen. Quick as a flash the senior chef took the dish out of the oven and tipped it onto the floor.

"Oh dear," he said, "accidents do happen—they'll have to have ice cream instead." And with a smile he walked off to inform the page of the "soufflé accident." Far better the Queen was told about a kitchen accident than to have her complain to the head chef in London about having been served a less-than-perfect soufflé.

Depending on the skill (and sobriety) of the senior chef, the junior chefs were rarely allowed to prepare the royal food. Maybe they would do a salad or perhaps vegetables. It was really an opportunity for a senior cook to stand out among the cadres of chefs who work for the Queen. I've seen fellow chefs, myself included, get quite puffed up when the page called the head chef in London on a Monday morning to say the Queen had really enjoyed the food that weekend.

Maids-a-Milking

There are two enormous parks that surround Windsor Castle, the Windsor Great Park and the Home Park. The Home Park is split into two parks by name—Home Park Public and Home Park Private. The latter is the Queen's private backyard. There she can drive and walk freely. It is also the home of the Windsor dairy, mausoleum, and gardens.

A dairy herd has been part of the castle's landscape for more than a century. Today there are two main breeds of cattle kept at Windsor: Jersey and Ayrshire. Carefully tended, the herds yield some of the best milk and cream found anywhere in England.

Milking takes place twice a day in the royal dairy. The dairy is a relatively new feature at Windsor. It was built in 1858 under the direction of Prince Albert, using advanced technology for its time. The main innovation is the use of double walls to keep the dairy cool, a must in the days before refrigeration. Although the milking process has changed over the years—it's no longer done by hand—the creamery remains the same.

It has a beautiful painted ceiling supported by six pillars and all of the walls are decorated with ornate tiles. Two tables covered in thick marble stretch the length of the room and more tables surround the edge of the room. All the original separating basins are in place and scattered around the marble tops. The original cream jugs are also still there, which were used to transport cream from the dairy to the castle.

When I worked at Windsor, the cream was still separated by hand. Mrs. Williams, the milkmaid, would hand spin the milk a gallon at a time using an old separator. Eight pints of milk from the royal cows would produce one pint of royal cream. Using a hand method for milk separation took hours, and if there were an upcoming state visit or garden party, we chefs had to give the dairy advance warning. Both milk and cream were unpasteurized.

The cream was so thick that you could literally stand a spoon up in it. It was even thicker than Cornish clotted cream. Crème brûlée, which the

Milking basins line the dairy walls

royals loved, achieved a new level when made with Windsor cream. Even vanilla ice cream turned into a voluptuous treat. The extra milk is turned into cheese made in little three-inch

Decorative statuary displayed along with antique pitchers in the Home Park Private mausoleum. Notice the beautiful hand-painted tiles.

pots set in polystyrene boxes. The royal family loves it and they have it sent up to Balmoral during the summer for the lunchtime cheese boards.

There has been much discussion of late about pasteurization, especially in regard to cheesemaking. Cheese made with pasteurized milk often lacks the depth of flavor found in nonpasteurized or "raw" cheeses. It wasn't until 1990 that the Queen agreed to have the milk pasteurized for "safety reasons." All the royal chefs mourned this change and we agreed that some of the milk's incomparable taste was lost.

SPRINGTIME AT THE CASTLE

Certain rituals mark Windsor's year. In early spring, the entire Windsor family celebrates Easter with services at St. George's chapel. In June, the Order of the Garter ceremony takes place, an annual celebration of Britain's oldest and highest order of chivalry. For sports enthusiasts there are two big events: the Windsor Horse Show in May and Royal Ascot in June. The Queen also allows celebrity charity cricket matches to take place in Home Park, and there is the annual fiercely competitive match between the Lords Taverners Team and the Royal Household Cricket Team.

Windsor Mulberries

Beginning in the 1200s, English kings decided to attempt the production of silk on their own lands. Mulberry trees were imported and planted in hopes of providing silkworms with their favorite food. The cool, damp climate kept silk production low and sporadic, even though the trees flourished.

Stemming from that time, the walkway along the royal dairy is lined with beautiful mulberry trees. To a chef, mulberry trees mean mulberry gin. We would collect ripe mulberries from the ground under the trees, then wash and steep them in gin for several weeks. The gin takes on the flavor of the ripe berries and turns a gorgeous purple hue. It is a fine drink and, in my opinion, much superior to sloe gin, which we made from pricked sloe berries. After we tasted the mulberry gin to ensure it was properly steeped (very important tasting that was), it was sent to the royal cellars to be used for shooting lunches in the Scottish highlands and at Sandringham Castle.

Easter Traditions

The royal family doesn't celebrate Easter publicly, but enjoys the holiday as a private family affair with wonderful traditions. Of course, there are hot cross buns to eat on Good Friday and on Shrove Tuesday the Queen, as head of the Church of England and like the rest of Christian England, has pancakes for dinner, which are what

Americans would call "crepes." Two hot thin pancakes are filled with vanilla sugar, folded and served with lemon juice and cream. Prince Philip prefers his cold and filled with raspberry jam and whipped cream. These are called "Crepes Islandaise" or Icelandic pancakes because he was visiting Iceland when he first tasted them.

Pancake day meant making around seven hundred crepes for everyone. It sounds like a lot, but with crepe pans on each burner, it would actually go fairly quickly. There is a rhythm to making them, and once I got into that rhythm hot crepes seemed to fill every available surface around me. During one Christmas at Sandringham, I was manning my crepe pans on all six burners when the Queen and her sister, Princess Margaret, came into the kitchen. The Queen was headed for the larder section and Princess Margaret was headed toward me.

"Lillibet, come look at this!" the princess shouted to her sister.

Oh yes, I thought, *the Queen will be impressed watching me with six pans.*

Instead she said, "Isn't that cheating? Aren't you supposed to toss them?"

I quickly put down my spatula and tossed the first one. Increasingly nervous, I continued pouring and flipping and said a quick prayer under my breath that I didn't spill a pancake on the floor.

Happy Easter for children and grownups alike

They both continued to watch for a few minutes, and then satisfied, moved on.

The Queen gives up chocolate for Lent, so banished are her favorite Bendicks Bittermints and Charbonel et Walker chocolates. On Easter Sunday the chefs would go to great lengths to prepare all sorts of chocolate treats to make up for the forty days of abstinence. There were chocolate cakes plus milk chocolate, white chocolate, and bittersweet chocolate eggs. This trove of chocolate treats would be served at royal teatime for several days, before finding its way into the staff dining room. The Queen's birthday is shortly after Easter, and she celebrates each April 21 at Windsor with another lovely chocolate cake. It's a large twelve-inch cake layered with and covered in ganache. A simple "Happy Birthday" is handwritten on the top in royal icing.

The children in the nursery would also get some sugar mice to eat and special chocolate eggs illustrating a nursery tale or fable. One year I decided it would be "Hickory, Dickory, Dock." I labored over a twelve-inch hollow chocolate egg. Inserted into that egg was a sugar mouse with its head poking out, and on the front was a clock's face set at one o'clock—"as the mouse ran down." Prince William loved it and immediately bit off the mouse's head with gusto, transforming the egg from art to food in record time! The nanny sent it back to the kitchen, quickly saying that the headless mouse was distressing the younger children. I gave it a quick makeover with a new mouse and back up it went. All better.

Diana at the Castle

I always looked forward to seeing Princess Diana and the boys at the castle. The princess seemed to enjoy the break too. Often she would spend time visiting in the kitchen, chatting with me about the day and finding out what we were cooking for dinner.

The princess quite liked Windsor. It wasn't too far from London and, as she once said, she could get "passes" to sneak back to the city. One afternoon, I was walking my dogs in the Home Park and saw her car approaching. She spotted me, stopped the car, rolled her window down about two inches, and said, "Does the Queen know you keep wolves in her back garden, Darren?"

I laughed and the younger of my two German shepherds enthusiastically jumped up to her car window, wagging her tail. The princess let out a yelp and said good-bye before quickly driving off. The next morning, the Queen's page caught up with me and mentioned, "I hear you set your wolves onto Princess Diana yesterday."

Good Lord! I don't know who else she told. I realized then that she wasn't all that fond of dogs.

I always enjoyed Easter court at Windsor. Spring was just around the corner, the asparagus and lettuces were in season, and there was always a glorious lamb to roast for Easter lunch. On Sundays the Queen's garden was open to the public and a military band would play. Luckily, my room in Brunswick Tower looked right over the garden. In the afternoons I could sit there with the window open and listen to the music float up. Other days I would watch Princess Diana playing with the boys and having fun. It was a timeless scene of England.

The Order of the Garter

The Order of the Garter is the highest honor bestowed on a British citizen as a reward for loyalty to the Crown, military merit, or to those who have significantly contributed to English life. Appointments are made solely by the Queen, are for life, and are restricted to no more than twenty-four people at any time.

Every June, the Order gathers at Windsor Castle to invest any new members and to reaffirm their commitment. A lunch is given in the Waterloo chamber, which is one of Windsor's main dining rooms. It's an elegantly decorated room with a dining table set to match. The food is served on gilt plates, solid silver covered with a thin layer of gold. The members are dressed in traditional blue velvet robes and the mood is festive. For dessert the invitees have a traditional "pudding," one of my favorites: Framboises St. George. St. George is the patron saint of England and his image is closely connected with the Windsor family. The dessert mimics the flag of St. George, a red cross on a white field.

Before the Windsor fire in '92, there wasn't an elevator in the kitchen, so the food was collected on large mahogany trays with a footman on either end. The middle footmen carried a tray in each hand as they marched out. It looked like a train with its carriages leaving the kitchens.

Ascot

Windsor is perfectly suited for sports of all kinds. Some have a long and venerable history of play on the Windsor properties. Others are more recent. But none carries with it the cachet of the Royal Ascot races. It attracts aristocrats and rogues alike and is an immensely popular part of springtime at the castle. Even the Queen takes a keen interest in Ascot since she has some of her own horses running in the races.

The races take place around mid-June and racing goes on for four days. The racetrack, owned by the royal family, is not in the Great Park, but across town. My favorite day of the races is "Ladies Day," a throwback to the time when only men were allowed to bet on horses. Women show up in beautiful dresses with hats to match. I always tried to attend races that day, since my unscientific survey led me to believe that Ladies Day at Ascot held more stunning women per square inch than any place on earth.

Ascot is a busy time for chefs. The house is full, with at least fifteen to twenty members of the royal family, plus guests, in residence. There can be no dawdling over meals back at the castle, as the Queen is always in attendance in the royal box when the first race begins at 1:30 p.m. Lunch starts promptly at noon, and then the royal retinue piles into cars and drives halfway down the long walk, before getting out and switching to horse-drawn carriages for the rest of the journey across town. Making a grand entrance, the Queen's carriage arrives on the racetrack before moving into the royal enclosure—the best box seats in the world.

Ascot

The Queen is never more gleeful than when one of her horses comes in first at Ascot. She is a keen horsewoman and has always maintained her own racing stable with Lord Porchester as her racing manager. Typically there are about twenty-five thoroughbred horses in training at any given time, and the Queen knows each horse's lineage and racing times.

Ascot is about racing and betting. The royal family does place wagers, though the sums are fairly modest. Of course, the bets placed are higher when one of the Queen's horses takes to the tracks. It's easy to spot her horses. The Queen's jockeys stand out in their royal racing colors of purple, gold, and scarlet.

Close behind would be the Ascot van that held all the food the family and guests would enjoy while watching the races. The van was loaded with Ascot boxes, three-foot-tall wooden boxes with a door on one side. Inside each box was room for six trays of food. The larder chef would pack the trays with at least two different kinds of tea sandwiches, cut small enough for a single bite. I would send three different kinds of tea cakes, scones, fresh ice cream, and the very popular iced coffee mixed with milk, sugar syrup, and Windsor cream, served in a huge thermos flask. We even had a recipe for it so that it tasted exactly the same for every Ascot and garden party. The tension of horse racing must stimulate the appetite, for I noticed that very little food came back uneaten.

Ascot kicked off the summer for palace chefs. Now we could use strawberries, cherries, and all the wonderful summer fruits. The Queen was quite particular about eating fruit in season. We could serve strawberries almost every day during the summer—but woe betide any chef who put them on the menu in January.

The Windsor hothouses grow white peaches that are absolutely beautiful to look at and even better to eat. Each peach is handpicked, wrapped individually in gauze, and stored in specially made crates. We could cook bruised peaches, but the unblemished beauties were eaten in their pristine state. Forget chocolate desserts when Windsor peaches were in season—a whole Windsor peach on your plate with a silver jug of Windsor dairy cream—bliss.

Windsor Horse Show

The Horse Show is a classic horse exhibition. There is show jumping—which the Queen and Princess Anne both took part in—Shetland pony races and carriage driving. One of the events much loved by the Duke of Edinburgh is the International Driving Grand Prix, an absolutely hair-raising competition of small phaetons led by four to six horses. The grand prix is always run individually and against the clock while traveling full bore through rough terrain. To the viewers it always seems like a miracle that horse and driver end up at the finish line in one piece. The Duke participates each year in the race and, even as a man now in his eighties, he shows no sign of "giving up the reins."

The staff at Windsor did not need to attend the show to know how the Duke was ranking. His disposition told all. If he was in a grumpy mood, then we knew that he was a lot further down in the rankings than he thought he should be. Same thing when he was competing in yacht races during Cowes Week on HMY *Britannia*. The only difference was that he would come into *Britannia's* galley kitchen and rant at the chefs. Good thing the kitchens at Windsor were farther away from the royal apartments!

The Windsor Horse Show

The Windsor Horse Show takes place in the private half of Home Park, typically around mid-May, and it highlights the equestrian activities that are part of the royal household. Attendance is open to the public, but participation is by royal invitation only. While some may argue it is not the best equestrian event in the country, most agree that with Windsor Castle as a backdrop it is the most impressive. At night the castle is floodlit and looks like a picturesque fairy tale.

Staff is offered one free ticket each to attend the show and most choose Sunday to catch the finale firework display. Some mates and I would head down to the show as soon as we had sent up royal dinner and changed out of our chef whites. My favorite part was the musical ride by the royal horse artillery and their finale when all six guns were first fired individually and then all together. It can be heard all over Windsor. We would then make a mad dash back up the hill to the castle and up onto the north terrace to watch the fireworks. From that terrace, we were at eye level and the display was amazing.

During the horse show, the house is full and many of the guests are friends of the Duke's or competitors in the events. One faithful guest is Count Andrassy, a close relation of the Windsors'. I would always make "Andrassy Pudding" as one of the special desserts during his stay. Basically, a chocolate soufflé, turned out and cooled, is sliced and filled with a really rich thick chocolate cream. The sides are coated with the chocolate cream and dusted with chocolate shavings. It is chocolaty and excessive and everyone eats it up. Even me.

SPRING ASPARAGUS SOUP WITH DILL

Soup

1   pound asparagus

1/2   stick (1/4 cup) unsalted butter

1/2   medium onion, finely chopped

1   tablespoon all-purpose flour

2   cups homemade or canned chicken broth

     Salt and freshly ground pepper

Dill oil

1/2   cup finely chopped fresh dill

1/4   cup olive oil

1   teaspoon lemon juice

     Salt and pepper

1. **For the soup**, cut the flowered top off of each asparagus spear, just about an inch long, and set these aside as a garnish for the finished soup. Chop the remaining asparagus spears into 1/2-inch pieces, discarding the bottom 2 inches of the woody stem. Melt the butter over a medium flame in a 4-quart pot. Add the onions and asparagus. Sauté until the onion is translucent and the asparagus begin to soften. Add the flour, and cook for 1 minute, stirring constantly. Add the chicken broth, and bring to a boil. Reduce the heat to a simmer, and cook for about 15 minutes.

2. While the soup is simmering, in a small saucepan bring 3 cups of water to a boil. Add the asparagus tips and blanch briefly. Drain the tips and run under cold water. The color should remain a bright green and the tips still crunchy for texture.

3. Taste the soup and add salt and pepper to taste. The asparagus should be fully cooked and rather soft. Puree the soup, using either a hand-held blender or a traditional blender. Once blended, pass the soup though a strainer into a clean bowl for a perfectly smooth texture. Return the pureed soup to a clean saucepan to reheat or refrigerate the soup until needed. The soup can be made a day ahead up to this point.

4. **For the dill oil**, put the dill, olive oil, lemon juice, salt, and pepper together in a blender until smooth and bright green in color. Adjust the seasonings, adding a bit more lemon juice or salt if the flavor is too neutral.

5. Reheat the soup slowly over a low flame, taking care not to boil. Ladle it into soup bowls or a tureen, and garnish with the reserved asparagus tips and a drizzle of dill oil.

MAKES 4 SERVINGS AS A FIRST COURSE

CUCUMBER AND MINT MOUSSE

1	English cucumber	1/2	cup plus 2 tablespoons chicken broth
	Salt	1	tablespoon finely chopped fresh mint
8	ounces cream cheese, softened		Freshly ground pepper
1/2	cup plus 2 tablespoons mayonnaise	1/2	cup plus 2 tablespoons heavy cream
1	packet Knox unflavored gelatin	1	lemon, juice only

1. Peel the cucumber, and cut it in half lengthways. Remove the seeds, and cut the flesh into 1/4-inch dice. Place in a colander, and sprinkle lightly with salt to taste. Leave for 1 hour to allow the salt to draw the liquid out of the cucumber. Squeeze the cucumber in a towel to extract any additional moisture.

2. In a mixing bowl or electric mixer, beat the cream cheese and the mayonnaise until the mixture is smooth. In a small saucepan, combine the gelatin with the chicken broth, and heat until the gelatin dissolves. Whisk the warm gelatin into the cream cheese mixture. Fold in the cucumber and chopped mint. Taste and adjust the salt and ground pepper to taste. Set aside until the mixture begins to thicken, about 30 minutes.

3. Whip the heavy cream into soft peaks (do not overbeat), and fold it gently into the thickened cucumber mixture. Add the lemon juice and stir gently. Pour the mousse into a terrine, ramekins, or a china soufflé dish, and refrigerate until firm. Decorate the top with thinly sliced, peeled cucumber halves. Serve with a green salad and chive cream dressing.

MAKES 6 SERVINGS

CHIVE CREAM DRESSING

1/4	Knorr chicken bouillon cube	2	tablespoons chopped fresh chives
1/4	cup water	1/2	lemon, juiced
1/2	cup mayonnaise		Salt and freshly ground pepper

1. In a small pan over a low heat, dissolve the bouillon cube in the water and then remove from the heat. Put the mayonnaise in a large bowl, and whisk in the warm broth. Add the chopped chives and lemon juice, and adjust the seasoning with the salt and pepper.

2. Refrigerate the dressing until needed. Keeps for up to three days.

MAKES 1 CUP

ROAST SPRING LEG OF LAMB

1 bone-in leg of lamb, 4 to 4½ pounds

6 cloves garlic, smashed

1 tablespoon fresh or dried rosemary

1 teaspoon fresh or dried thyme leaves

Kosher salt and coarsely ground black pepper

¼ cup olive oil

2 large carrots, cut into large pieces

1 large onion, peeled and cut into large pieces

3 ribs celery, cut into large pieces

1 tablespoon all-purpose flour

1½ cups chicken broth

1 cup red wine

1 bay leaf

1 tablespoon red currant jelly

1. Preheat the oven to 400 degrees. Remove the lamb from the refrigerator, and allow it to come to room temperature. Rub the garlic, rosemary, and thyme all over the lamb, and season liberally with the salt and pepper. Heat the oil in a large roasting pan over high heat. Carefully place the lamb into the roasting pan, and, using tongs, sear all sides of the meat until golden brown. Remove the lamb from the roasting pan and set aside.

2. Reduce the heat to medium, and add the carrots, onions, and celery to the roasting pan. Stir briefly. Make a bed with the vegetables, and place the leg of lamb on top of the vegetables. Place the roasting pan in the center of the oven. Roast the lamb for 45 minutes uncovered and then an additional 45 minutes covered with aluminum foil until it reaches an internal temperature of 160 degrees to 170 degrees. Remove the lamb from the oven, and lift it onto a clean plate. Allow the roast to rest, covered, for about 20 minutes.

3. Carefully strain off most of the excess fat from the roasting pan. You should have about ¼ cup left in the bottom along with the vegetables. Return the pan to the stovetop, and over low heat, add the flour and stir. Next stir in the chicken broth and red wine, and add the bay leaf and red currant jelly. Increase the heat, bring the sauce to a boil, and adjust the seasoning. Pour any accumulated juices from the lamb into the sauce. Remove the vegetables to a warm serving platter, and strain the sauce into a sauceboat. Slice the meat thinly and serve with the sauce and vegetables.

MAKES 6 TO 8 SERVINGS

BEEF WELLINGTON

½	stick (¼ cup) butter	¼	teaspoon celery seeds
2	teaspoons salt, divided	1	3-pound, center-cut beef tenderloin
1	small onion, finely chopped	¼	cup olive oil
1	pound portabella mushrooms, blended to paste in a food processor	1	(14-ounce) box Dufour classic puff pastry *or* 1 (17-ounce) box Pepperidge Farm puff pastry
¼	cup heavy cream	8	ounces foie gras, or a good liver pâté
1	tablespoon Worcestershire sauce	1	egg, beaten
1	teaspoon coarsely ground black pepper		
½	teaspoon English mustard powder		

1. Preheat the oven to 400 degrees. Heat a large sauté pan over medium heat. Add ½ stick butter, 1 teaspoon salt, and the onion. Sauté until the onion is softened and translucent. Add the mushrooms to the sauté pan, and cook until they have released all their liquid and the pan is relatively dry. Add the cream and Worcestershire sauce, and cook until reduced and the mixture has formed a smooth paste. Check the mixture for seasoning, and set aside to cool.

2. In a small bowl, mix together the remaining teaspoon of salt, the black pepper, mustard powder, and celery seeds. Rub the spice mixture on all sides of the tenderloin. In a nonstick frying pan large enough to hold the tenderloin, heat the olive oil until it starts to smoke. Sear the beef on all sides. Remove and let the beef cool completely.

3. Roll out the puff pastry into a rectangle large enough to enclose the beef tenderloin with the long side parallel to your body. Spread the cooled mushroom mixture over the pastry, leaving at least 3 inches around the edges. Slice the foie gras or liver paté, and lay it down the horizontal center of the pastry. Place the tenderloin on top.

4. Brush the long edges of the pastry with some beaten egg, and fold over the mushroom mixture and tenderloin, tucking in the ends. Press the edges together to seal. Place the tenderloin seam side down on a baking sheet, and brush the top and sides of the pastry with the remaining beaten egg.

5. Bake the tenderloin for 10 minutes. Reduce the heat to 350 degrees, and cook for 20 minutes longer, or until the pastry is golden brown. Remove from the oven, and allow the beef to rest for at least 5 minutes before slicing. Trim off the ends of the pastry, and cut into six even slices to serve. Beef Wellington can be accompanied by a Madeira wine sauce or a classic Hollandaise.

MAKES 6 SERVINGS

Beef Wellington, Choux à la Cherbourg

CHOUX À LA CHERBOURG

(cabbage in a creamy garlic and bacon sauce)

This is a great way to use up leftover cabbage and it delivers fabulous flavor. As this bubbles away in the oven, the cream thickens and a garlic aroma fills the kitchen.

1	large Savoy cabbage, about 3 pounds	6	cloves garlic, sliced
1	tablespoon salt plus additional salt for seasoning as needed	3	cups heavy cream
			Freshly ground black pepper
6	slices thickly cut bacon, diced	1	cup grated Parmesan cheese

1. Preheat the oven to 350 degrees. Remove the outer leaves of the cabbage, cut the cabbage in half, remove the core, and roughly chop the remaining leaves. Fill a saucepan with water, add 1 tablespoon salt, and bring to a boil. The pot should be large enough to hold all the cabbage. When the water boils, add the cabbage, and let simmer until it is fork tender, about 15 minutes.

2. While the cabbage is cooking, sauté the bacon in a frying pan until crispy. Remove the bacon onto a paper towel to cool and drain. Add the garlic to the same pan, and sauté it in the bacon fat until soft. Remove the garlic and add it to the crispy bacon.

3. Heat the cream in a heavy, nonstick pan, and allow it to reduce by half. Let cool. Once the cabbage is tender, drain it through a colander, and press down with a plate to remove any excess moisture. Turn the cabbage out onto a chopping board, and again roughly chop the cooked cabbage.

4. In a medium-sized casserole dish, add the cabbage and sprinkle the bacon and garlic mixture over the top. Pour the cream over the cabbage, dust with salt and pepper to taste, and top with Parmesan cheese. Place the casserole in the oven for 20 minutes, or until the cabbage is hot and bubbling and the cheese has melted.

MAKES 6 TO 8 SERVINGS

ROASTED SPRING VEGETABLES

2	pounds small red-skin potatoes, washed and quartered	3/4	cup olive oil
2	pounds carrots, cut into 3/4-inch rounds	2	cloves garlic, crushed
		1	tablespoon kosher salt
4	large fennel bulbs	2	teaspoons freshly ground black pepper
2	leeks, cleaned and sliced into 1/2-inch rounds	1	bunch fresh tarragon, finely chopped

1. Preheat the oven to 350 degrees. Place the potatoes and carrots in a large mixing bowl. Trim the fennel bulbs of any brown outer leaves, and chop off the fronds. You just want to use the bulb here. Cut the bulbs in half vertically, and then cut each half into vertical 1/2-inch wedges. Add the fennel and leeks to the mixing bowl with the potatoes and carrots.

2. In a separate smaller bowl, add the oil, garlic, salt, and pepper, and whisk to combine. Pour this mixture over the vegetables and stir, coating all the vegetables well. Transfer the contents to a baking sheet, and bake the vegetables for 45 minutes to 1 hour, or until they are tender and slightly browned around the edges.

3. Spoon the vegetables onto a serving platter, and garnish with the chopped tarragon before serving.

MAKES 6 TO 8 SERVINGS

Roasted Spring Vegetables (left), Normandy-Style Boulangère Potatoes (front), Petit Pois à la Français (French-style peas) (top)

NORMANDY-STYLE BOULANGÈRE POTATOES

Boulangère potatoes are enjoyed all across France. They date back to the days when people didn't have ovens in the home. Wives would slice the potatoes and onions into a clearly labeled casserole dish and stop by the local boulangère *(baker) on their way to church on a Sunday morning. The baker, who had just finished making the day's bread and whose ovens were still hot, would charge a small fee to cook the potatoes and often a leg of lamb. This would be collected on the way home from church and be the centerpiece of the family's Sunday feast.*

This potato dish is considered "Normandy-style" because of its use of leeks. Normandy, in northern France, is famous for its rolling countryside, orchards full of apples (read Calvados), and fields of leeks. It is the leeks, however, that transform this classic dish into something regional and spectacular. Use a good quality smoked bacon.

4	large Russet potatoes, about 2 pounds
1	large leek, rinsed and thinly sliced
4	slices raw bacon, diced
2	tablespoons finely chopped garlic
	Salt and freshly ground pepper
1	teaspoon dried or fresh thyme
2	cups homemade or canned chicken broth
1/2	stick (4 tablespoons) butter, melted
1	tablespoon finely chopped fresh parsley

1. Preheat the oven to 350 degrees. Peel and finely slice the potatoes to about 1/8 inch thick. Lay one-third of the potatoes in an ovenproof baking dish. Add half of the sliced leeks, the diced bacon, and chopped garlic. Season with salt and pepper to taste, and sprinkle on the thyme. Make a second layer using one-third of the potatoes, and the remaining leeks, bacon, and garlic. Again season with salt and pepper to taste. Top with the remaining potatoes, overlapping and arranging them in a decorative pattern.

2. Pour the chicken broth over the potatoes, and brush the top layer with the melted butter. Cover with aluminum foil, and bake for about 1 hour. Remove the foil during the last 20 minutes of baking to allow the top layer of potatoes to brown and get crispy. Sprinkle with the parsley and serve.

MAKES 4 SERVINGS

PETIT POIS À LA FRANÇAIS

(French-style peas)

Freshly shelled peas brought to boil and served with butter and chopped fresh mint are delicious through the spring and summer months. But these French-style peas are also a great way of using frozen peas and are a fine alternative in this recipe, which employs a traditional braising method. In times past, the peas would be stewed for so long they would turn grey. They still tasted good, however.

6	slices bacon, diced		1	pinch freshly ground pepper
1	large onion, thinly sliced		1	chicken bouillon cube
1/4	head iceberg lettuce, shredded		2	cups water (or enough to cover)
1 1/2	pounds frozen green peas		2	tablespoons unsalted butter, softened
1	teaspoon salt		3	tablespoons all-purpose flour
3	tablespoons sugar		1	small bunch fresh mint, chopped

1. In a 2-quart saucepan over medium heat, fry the bacon slowly until it is soft and some of the fat has been rendered. Stir in the sliced onions and lettuce, and let them simmer for about 5 minutes. Add the peas, salt, sugar, pepper, chicken bouillon cube, and water to cover. Continue to cook slowly until the bouillon cube has dissolved and the peas are heated through and done to the desired degree of firmness, about 5 to 10 minutes.

2. Meanwhile, in a small mixing bowl, combine the butter and flour. Add the butter and flour mixture to the peas and bring to a boil. Remove from the heat and stir. Garnish with mint and serve immediately.

MAKES 6 SERVINGS

POMMES FONDANTES

Fondant potatoes are nothing more than roasted potatoes that are simmered in a small amount of broth until they are tender. Usually the potatoes are cut in a classic shape, called "tournes," where you trim each piece into a barrel shape. I've simplified that by just calling for the potatoes to be cut in equal sizes. By finishing the potatoes in broth it gives them a longer hold time—you can prepare them ahead of time and reheat them when you are ready.

2	large Russet potatoes, about 14 ounces	1 1/2	to 2 cups homemade or canned chicken broth or vegetable broth
1/2	stick (1/4 cup) unsalted butter	1	sprig fresh thyme
			Salt and freshly ground pepper

Preheat the oven to 350 degrees. Peel and cut the potatoes into even-size shapes, approximately 3 inches in length, 2 1/2 inches in width. In a sauté pan large enough to hold the potatoes in one layer, melt the butter over a low heat, add the potatoes, and cook slowly until they are golden brown on all sides. This will take 15 to 20 minutes.

DILL CREAM SAUCE

4	tablespoons unsalted butter	1	cup water
1	cup sliced button mushrooms	1	cup white wine or 1 extra cup water
1	cup finely diced onions	1	chicken bouillon cube
3	cloves garlic, crushed	1	lemon, juiced
1/4	cup all-purpose flour	1/2	cup chopped fresh dill
			Salt and freshly ground pepper

Melt the butter in a heavy-bottomed saucepan until hot, but not smoking. Add the mushrooms, onions, and garlic. Sauté until the onions start to soften. Stir in the flour, then the water, wine, and bouillon cube. Simmer for 10 minutes or until the mixture thickens to a sauce consistency. Add the lemon juice, dill, and salt and pepper. Taste to correct seasonings.

MAKES 6 SERVINGS

VANILLA ICE CREAM

This is my base recipe. You can keep it as vanilla, but could also melt eight ounces of chocolate in a bowl and then pour it over the ice cream base as soon as it coats the back of the spoon. Whisk and then chill. For coffee ice cream, add one tablespoon of instant coffee to the egg and sugar mix. It will dissolve when the boiling milk is poured on it. To get something like the quality of ice cream we used at Windsor with milk from the royal dairies, I whisk in a six-ounce jar of English clotted cream to the chilled base. Then you are ready to freeze it into a remarkable bowl of ice cream.

6 egg yolks
1 whole egg
1/2 cup vanilla sugar (see page 76)
2 1/2 cups whole milk

1 vanilla bean or 1 teaspoon vanilla extract
1 1/4 cups heavy cream

1. In a large mixing bowl, beat the egg yolks, whole egg, and vanilla sugar until the mixture starts to lighten in color. At the same time, put the milk and vanilla bean or vanilla extract into a heavy saucepan, and bring the milk to a simmer over a low flame. Remove the milk from the heat as soon as it simmers, and very slowly pour it onto the egg mixture, whisking all the time. This slow pour ensures that the egg yolks don't curdle.

2. Return the milk, egg, and sugar mixture back to the saucepan on the stove over low heat. Slowly cook the mixture, stirring constantly with a wooden spoon over the whole bottom of the pan until the milk thickens enough to coat the back of a wooden spoon. It should have a thick, creamy consistency.

3. Strain the mixture through a sieve to break up any lumps, and pour it into a clean bowl. Refrigerate until cold. If you have used a vanilla pod, remove it now and split it down the middle. Scrape out the seeds into the custard mixture.

4. When the custard is completely cold, whisk the heavy cream to soft peaks and fold it into the custard. Pour the custard into an electric ice cream machine, and churn following the manufacturer's instructions.

MAKES 8 SERVINGS

ANDRASSY PUDDING

If you've been afraid of making soufflés, this is a great recipe to begin with. If it doesn't rise properly, it's okay, because you are going to let it sink again before you serve it. Eventually you will be making the most amazing chocolate soufflés and will want to rush them to the table to impress your guests, rather than letting them sink and go cold for this dish.

2 tablespoons unsalted butter (for greasing the soufflé dish), softened

Soufflé

1/4 cup (1/2 stick) unsalted butter

1/3 cup granulated sugar

1/3 cup cocoa powder

1/4 cup all-purpose flour

1 1/4 cups milk

6 eggs, separated

Frosting

1/4 cup (1/2 stick) unsalted butter

1/3 cup granulated sugar

1/3 cup cocoa powder

1/4 cup all-purpose flour

1 1/4 cups milk

6 egg yolks

1 (4-ounce) bar Ghirardelli milk chocolate, finely grated

Whipped cream

1. Preheat the oven to 400 degrees and place a baking rack onto the middle shelf of the oven. Make sure the top rack is removed to allow room for the soufflé to rise. Grease an 8-inch soufflé dish with the butter, leaving a lip of butter all along the top edge.

2. **For the soufflé,** prepare the base by melting the butter in a heavy saucepan and adding the sugar, cocoa powder, and flour. Whisk until combined, and then gradually incorporate the milk to form a smooth sauce. Remove from the heat, and whisk in the egg yolks. Pour the mixture into a large bowl, and allow it to cool for about 15 minutes.

3. In a separate bowl, whip the egg whites until stiff, and fold them into the soufflé base. Spoon the mixture into the prepared soufflé dish, and bake for 18 minutes or until well risen. Remove the soufflé from the oven and set it on a cooling rack. Allow the soufflé to cool and sink. While it is still warm, turn the soufflé out onto the cooling rack, and let it cool completely.

4. **For the frosting**, melt the butter in a heavy-bottomed saucepan. Add the sugar, cocoa powder, and flour, and whisk until combined. Gradually incorporate the milk to form a smooth sauce. Remove from the heat and whisk in the egg yolks. Pour the mix into a large bowl, cover with plastic wrap, and allow the soufflé to cool.

5. Slice the soufflé in half horizontally, creating two layers, and spread some of the

frosting onto the bottom layer. Replace the top layer and spread the remaining frosting over the top and sides of the soufflé. Place the soufflé carefully onto a serving plate, and sprinkle the finely grated chocolate onto the top and sides of the pudding. Serve with whipped cream.

MAKES 10 SERVINGS

CREPES ISLANDAISE

The Duke of Edinburgh was served this dish on a state visit to Iceland. He enjoyed it so much that he asked for the recipe and royal chefs have been making these crepes ever since.

1 cup all-purpose flour	1 teaspoon vanilla paste
1/4 teaspoon baking powder	1/2 stick (1/4 cup) unsalted butter, melted
1/4 teaspoon salt	1/4 cup seedless raspberry jam
1/2 teaspoon baking soda	1 cup heavy cream, whipped
3 eggs	2 tablespoons powdered sugar, for dusting
2 1/2 cups milk	

1. Sift the flour, baking powder, salt, and soda into a large bowl. In a separate bowl, mix the eggs, milk, and vanilla paste. Add the egg and milk mixture to the dry ingredients, and stir until combined.

2. Add the melted butter a little at a time to an 8-inch crepe pan or frying pan, and heat over high heat. Spoon about 2 tablespoons of the batter into the pan, and allow it to spread and set. Flip the crepe over to cook the other side, and when done, remove it to a plate to cool slightly. This whole process should take less than a minute. Repeat with the rest of the batter.

3. Spread the jam over the top of each pancake, and add a spoonful of whipped cream. Fold the pancake in half twice so that you have a neat triangle, and dust it with the powdered sugar. Serve immediately.

MAKES 6 SERVINGS

COFFEE MOUSSE

I can't tell you how many times we forgot to send the chocolate covered coffee beans down to Windsor in the Ascot boxes on a Friday. It was then a frantic rush to find any Buckingham Palace staff that lived at Windsor to "drop by the castle kitchen" on their way home. More often than not, the beans would be used to create this coffee mousse. It is the perfect make-ahead dessert that looks quite elegant but is dead easy. Buy more than you need of the chocolate covered coffee beans—you can snack while you're working.

1 packet Knox unflavored gelatin	3/4 cup heavy cream
1¼ cups whole milk, divided	2 egg whites
2 egg yolks	1/2 cup dark chocolate-covered coffee beans, divided
1/3 cup granulated sugar	Whipped cream
1 teaspoon instant coffee granules	

1. In a bowl large enough to hold all the ingredients, dissolve the gelatin in ¼ cup cold milk. In a separate bowl, add the egg yolks, sugar, and instant coffee. Whisk until combined. Bring the remaining 1 cup milk to the boil in a heavy-bottomed saucepan, and slowly pour it onto the egg mixture, whisking constantly. Return the mixture to the saucepan, and over low heat, stir until the mixture starts to thicken and coat the back of the spoon. Remove from the heat, and pour the mixture over the gelatin. Whisk until all ingredients are combined. Strain the coffee custard mixture into a large bowl, and refrigerate until cold and starting to set.

2. In a large bowl, whip the cream until stiff. In another bowl, whip the egg whites until stiff. Alternating with the whipped cream, carefully fold the egg whites into the coffee custard. Spoon half the mixture into a six-cup serving dish, and sprinkle ¼ cup chocolate coffee beans on top. Cover with the remaining custard. Refrigerate the mousse until firm.

3. To serve, garnish with rosettes of whipped cream and the remaining ¼ cup chocolate coffee beans sprinkled over the top.

MAKES 6 SERVINGS

BRANDY SNAPS

These light, crunchy tuile-like rolled cookies are a popular tea cake and dessert. Using a star tip I would pipe whipped cream into half of the brandy snaps and the other half I would send up plain, without cream. Other times I would shape the brandy snaps around cream horn molds (cones) and make brandy snap cornets. These would be arranged neatly into a glass finger bowl and then filled with ice cream for the royal table. I think that is the closest the Queen ever came to eating ice cream out of a cone.

The brandy snaps can also be shaped around a tartlet mold to create a basket for sliced fruit. In that case, I would usually brush the inside with melted chocolate and let it set hard first. It stops the cookie from getting soggy when you serve it.

Golden syrup has the consistency of corn syrup and has a clear golden color. It's made from evaporated sugar cane juice and has a rich flavor. A good substitute is King brand syrup, a mixture of corn and invert sugar syrup that is widely sold throughout the United States. Corn syrup will work too, but will not give the golden color.

½ cup Demerara sugar (turbinado sugar will work as an alternative)	1 stick (8 tablespoons) unsalted butter
	1⅛ cups all-purpose flour
8 tablespoons golden syrup	1 teaspoon ground ginger

1. Preheat the oven to 350 degrees. In a medium-size, heavy-bottomed saucepan, melt the sugar, syrup, butter, flour, and ginger together over a low heat until combined. Be careful not to overheat; the mix just needs to be hot enough to melt the butter. Grease a large baking sheet or use a silpat nonstick baking sheet.

2. Spoon a heaping tablespoon of the cookie mix onto the baking sheet, leaving about 6 inches between each one to allow for the mixture to spread. Bake for 6 minutes, or until golden brown; then remove the baking sheet from the oven, and let the brandy snaps cool just slightly.

3. When the brandy snaps have set, but are still warm and can be easily lifted off the baking sheet, quickly ease one at a time off with a flat metal spatula and roll around a ¾-inch wooden dowel or a wooden spoon handle to create cylinders. Place on a baking rack to harden completely, about 2 minutes, and then ease them off the wooden spoon.

4. Repeat the process. If the brandy snaps start to break as you roll them, return the tray to the oven for a few minutes and they will soften again.

MAKES ABOUT 30 SNAPS

CRÈME BRÛLÉE

This is one of Prince Andrew's favorite desserts. Often it would be served with Sandringham oranges. The natural acidity of the oranges would balance the sweetness of the brûlée. For a change we would sometimes put peeled grapes on the bottom of the brûlée before baking and give it a fancy new name—Crème Brûlée au Raisin.

6   egg yolks

4   tablespoons granulated sugar

1   vanilla pod or ½ teaspoon vanilla extract

2   cups heavy cream

4   tablespoons granulated vanilla sugar (see page 76) for topping

1. Preheat the oven to 325 degrees. In a large mixing bowl, beat the egg yolks and sugar until they turn a light yellow color. Add the vanilla pod or extract.

2. In a separate heavy-bottomed saucepan, bring the heavy cream to a simmer. Once heated, immediately remove it from the heat, and slowly pour it into the egg yolk and sugar mixture, whisking constantly.

3. Put the liquid back into the saucepan set over low heat, and whisk or stir the milk mixture as it cooks, remembering to stir across the whole surface of the pan to keep the developing custard from forming lumps. Keep stirring until the custard thickens to the consistency of heavy cream. (Don't be impatient; this sometimes takes a while.) This custard does most of its cooking on top of the stove, not in the oven, so you really want it to be quite thick at this point.

4. Strain the custard into a clean bowl. If you used a vanilla pod, remove it, split it open, and scrape the seeds from inside the pod into the custard.

5. Divide the custard equally among six small ramekins. Place the ramekins in a larger pan, and fill the pan with hot tap water halfway up the sides of the ramekins.

6. Bake in the oven for 15 minutes, or until the custard jiggles like Jell-O when you give it a gentle shake. Remove the ramekins from the water bath, and let them cool completely in the refrigerator for at least 3 hours.

7. To serve, lightly sprinkle the tops of each ramekin with granulated vanilla sugar, and place them under a hot broiler until the sugar caramelizes, watching carefully so not to let the sugar burn.

MAKES 6 SERVINGS

ENGLISH PANCAKES

English pancakes are different from American pancakes. They are much thinner and contain no leavening. They are closer to a French crepe, only slightly thicker. Traditionally they are served on Shrove Tuesday, but are enjoyed year-round. They are best served straight from the pan. In my house the race is to try to make them faster than my children can eat them.

2 cups all-purpose flour	2 1/2 cups milk
1 1/2 tablespoons extra-fine granulated sugar	2 tablespoons vegetable oil, divided
Pinch of salt	1/2 stick (1/4 cup) unsalted butter
1 egg	Granulated sugar, lemons, and oranges for garnish
2 egg yolks	

1. In a large mixing bowl, whisk together the flour, sugar, and salt. Add the egg and egg yolks, followed by the milk and 1 tablespoon of the vegetable oil. Continue whisking until there are no lumps. In a separate small saucepan, melt the butter until it is golden brown, and whisk it into the pancake mix. Leave the batter to rest for about 15 minutes.

2. Heat an 8-inch frying pan until hot, and add the remaining 1 tablespoon vegetable oil, tilting the pan to spread the oil across the bottom. When the oil starts to smoke, pour the excess into a small bowl for later use. Return the pan to the heat. You now have a sheer coating of oil remaining on the pan.

3. Pour 2 tablespoons of the batter into the pancake pan, tilting the pan to coat the bottom evenly. Cook until the underside of the pancake is golden brown, and then, using a spatula, turn it over and cook the other side. Turn the pancake out onto an upturned dinner plate. Repeat until there is no more batter, using a bit of the reserved oil if the pan appears to be dry, or if the pancakes begin to stick. Continue to stack pancakes on top of each other on your dinner plate.

4. When finished, serve the pancakes straightaway with the sugar for sprinkling and the lemon and orange wedges on the side for squeezing on the pancakes.

5. If you want to make the pancakes in advance, lightly butter an ovenproof tray, and sprinkle each pancake with sugar after you finish cooking it. Fold the pancakes in half and then half again, arranging them all neatly on the tray. Cover the tray with foil and bake at 350 degrees for about 15 minutes. Serve with the lemon and orange wedges.

MAKES 20 (8-INCH) PANCAKES

CHOCOLATE PERFECTION PIE

Pastry

1¼ cups all-purpose flour

¼ cup sugar or vanilla sugar (see page 76)

1 stick (8 tablespoons) cold unsalted butter

1 egg yolk, beaten

2 tablespoons heavy cream

Filling

2 eggs

1 teaspoon ground cinnamon, divided

½ cup sugar

½ teaspoon white wine vinegar

¼ teaspoon salt

6 ounces (about 1½ bars) Ghirardelli semisweet chocolate

½ cup water

2 egg yolks

1 cup heavy cream

2 ounces Ghirardelli white chocolate, grated

1. Preheat the oven to 350 degrees.

2. **For the pastry dough**, pulse the flour and sugar a few times, just to mix, in a food processor fitted with a metal blade. Cut the chilled butter into cubes and add it to the flour mixture. Pulse briefly until the mixture forms little balls like moist crumbs with no visible chunks of butter.

3. Add the egg yolk and heavy cream and pulse again until a paste forms. Wrap the dough in plastic. Form it into a flattened ball and refrigerate for at least 30 minutes.

4. Roll out the pastry dough, and line a 9-inch tart ring. Prick the tart all over. Gently place a piece of parchment paper on the tart, and fill it with either tart weights or dried beans. Place the tart shell on the center rack of the oven for about 15 minutes. Remove the weights and parchment paper and return to bake for an additional 5 to 10 minutes, or until the crust is lightly colored and the base of the tart cooked.

5. **For the filling**, place a mixing bowl over a saucepan of simmering water. The bowl should not touch the water, but just be warmed by the steam. Add the eggs, ½ teaspoon cinnamon, sugar, vinegar, and salt. Whisk until the mixture starts to thicken and appears foamy. Remove the bowl from the top of the pan to a cool surface. Continue whisking until the mixture falls in slightly thick and creamy ribbons from your whisk.

Chocolate Perfection Pie

6. Pour the filling into the partially baked tart and return the tart to the oven. Bake for 15 minutes, or until the filling has risen and is firm to the touch. Remove the tart from the oven and place it on a cooling rack. Let the filling sink back into the shell. This is the first layer.

7. While the tart is cooling, melt the semisweet chocolate, and whisk in the water and egg yolks until combined. Spoon half of this chocolate mix over the top of the tart's sunken filling. Return the tart to the oven for an additional 5 minutes. Remove the tart from the oven and allow to cool completely. This is the second layer.

8. Whip the cream and remaining cinnamon until stiff peaks form, and carefully spread half of the whipped cream on top of the tart. This is the third layer.

9. Fold the remaining half of the whipped cream and cinnamon into the remaining melted chocolate and spread it on top. This is the fourth layer. Sprinkle on the grated white chocolate and refrigerate until set, about 1 hour.

MAKES 8 SERVINGS

ROYAL BIRTHDAY CAKE

Any leftover frosting can be chilled, then rolled into balls and dipped in cocoa powder, coconut, or nibbed almonds. Eat these truffles outright or use them to decorate the top of your cake.

Filling

1	pound Ghirardelli semisweet chocolate, chopped and divided
2	cups (1 pint) heavy cream, divided

Sponge cake

6	egg yolks
2	eggs
1/2	cup sugar
1/3	cup plus 2 teaspoons all-purpose flour
4	tablespoons Dutch cocoa powder
1/2	stick (1/4 cup) unsalted butter, melted and cooled

1. **For the filling,** prepare it at least six hours before baking the cake. Put half the chopped chocolate into a mixing bowl. In a separate saucepan, bring half the heavy cream to a simmer. Pour the hot cream onto the chocolate, letting the chocolate melt. Whisk it until smooth and well incorporated. Refrigerate until it cools and thickens to the consistency of a spreadable icing.

2. Preheat the oven to 350 degrees.

3. **For the cake,** butter an 8-inch round cake pan and line it with buttered parchment paper. Set a metal mixing bowl over a saucepan half filled with simmering water. The water shouldn't touch the bottom of the mixing bowl. Add the egg yolks, eggs, and sugar to the mixing bowl, and whisk together, allowing the heat from the simmering water to warm the mixture. In a separate bowl, sift the flour and cocoa together.

4. Keep whisking the egg mixture until it doubles in volume. Gently fold in the flour and cocoa mixture. Then fold in the cooled butter. Spoon the cake batter into the prepared cake pan, and bake for 20 minutes, or until the cake springs back slightly when pressed. Remove the cake from the oven onto a cooling rack.

5. **For the topping**, put the remaining half of the chopped chocolate into a mixing bowl. In a separate saucepan, bring the remaining heavy cream to a simmer. Pour the hot cream onto the chocolate, letting the chocolate melt. Whisk it until smooth and well incorporated, and then set it aside while you assemble the cake.

The Queen's birthday tea: Scones, Royal Birthday Cake, tea sandwiches, Raspberry Tartlets

6. **For the assembly**, slice the sponge cake into three horizontal layers. Place the bottom layer on a cooling rack. Using the refrigerated icing, top the bottom discs with a thick layer of icing, and then add the next layer of sponge cake and another thick layer of icing. Place the top of the cake over the second layer of icing.

7. Ladle the warm chocolate icing over the top of the sponge cake, allowing it to run down the sides. Cool the cake for at least 2 hours before decorating with chocolate.

MAKES 10 SERVINGS

VANILLA SUGAR

Vanilla beans, or pods as we call them in England, are expensive, but using them this way makes them very economical and they will last a year. The best ones are Tahitian and Bourbon. I like to use the Bourbon pods because they are a lot sweeter and contain more seeds. Both work well in this recipe, just make sure the ones you buy are oily to touch, smell fragrant, and are not brittle or dry.

5 cups granulated sugar
4 vanilla beans

1. Pour the sugar into an 8-cup Tupperware container with a tight fitting lid. Lay one of the beans flat on a chopping board and hold one end. Carefully cut open the bean down the center lengthwise, and scrape out the tiny black seeds. Place the bean and seeds into the sugar; repeat the process with all of the beans.

2. Place the lid on the container, and cover with plastic wrap. Shake the container for about a minute, and store in the pantry for at least a week. The sugar is now ready to use. Remember that if you take 1 tablespoon of vanilla sugar out of the container, you must replace it with 1 tablespoon of regular granulated sugar, and then shake the container again. This will maintain your source of vanilla sugar for about 1 year. After that, you will need to purchase more beans.

3. Serve the sugar in a small bowl with whipped cream alongside fresh strawberries, sprinkle it over a crème brûlée, and use it in baking.

MAKES 5 CUPS

LEMON MILLE-FEUILLE WITH RHUBARB COULIS

1   box phyllo dough (12 ounces)
1   egg, beaten
1/2 pound rhubarb, about 4 sticks
1   cup water
1/2 cup plus 1 tablespoon
    granulated sugar

1   quarter-size slice fresh ginger, peeled
1   recipe lemon cheese (recipe page 80)
1   tablespoon powdered sugar,
    for garnish

Lemon Mille-Feuille with Rhubarb Coulis

1. Preheat the oven to 350 degrees. Unroll the phyllo dough and lay out one sheet. Brush with the beaten egg and lay another sheet on top. Repeat so that you have three sheets thick. Using a 3-inch round cookie cutter, cut out 18 disks. Use more phyllo sheets if needed. Transfer the disks to a cookie sheet, and bake for about 8 minutes or until golden brown. Remove to a cooling rack.

2. **For the coulis,** wipe the rhubarb clean with a paper towel and trim the edges. Cut the rhubarb into 1/2-inch pieces and put them into a large pan. Add the water and 1/2 cup sugar and bring to a boil. Reduce to a simmer, stirring constantly, until the rhubarb softens. Strain the rhubarb, reserving the poaching liquid. Puree the rhubarb in a blender or food processor, adding a little of the reserved liquid until the rhubarb achieves a saucelike consistency. Smash the ginger to a fine pulp and add it to the rhubarb. Taste, adding the remaining 1 tablespoon sugar, if desired. Refrigerate for about 2 hours.

3. Build your mille feuille. Place a teaspoon of lemon cheese in the center of each plate and top with a disk of cooked phyllo. Add another teaspoon of lemon cheese followed by a second disk. Top with a third layer of lemon cheese and finish with another disk of cooked phyllo. Spoon the rhubarb coulis around the base of the mille feuille, dust the top disk of phyllo with powdered sugar, and serve.

MAKES 6 SERVINGS

FRAMBOISES ST. GEORGE

To make an authentic Raspberries St. George you need a rectangular dish like the one shown in the picture. This will make it easier for your guests to identify the Cross of St. George. By the way, the Cross of St. George is the true flag of England, not the Union flag as most everyone supposes. Of course, if you are not feeling compelled to create the English flag (and I do understand that might, on rare occasions, happen) you can assemble the ingredients in individual balloon wine glasses topped with fresh raspberries, fresh mint, and whipped cream. If you really want to impress your friends, serve this dish alongside Scottish Thistle Shortbread (recipe on page 131). Bet you don't have any leftovers!

If the raspberries are sad looking or you fancy a change, substitute fresh strawberries. Save the smaller ones for the cross in the middle.

1	quart (4 cups) fresh raspberries, divided	1	teaspoon vanilla paste
2	cups heavy cream		Whipped cream
1/2	cup granulated sugar		

1. Puree half (2 cups) of the fresh raspberries to a pulp. Strain them through a fine sieve to remove all seeds. In a large bowl whip the heavy cream with the granulated sugar and vanilla until stiff. Without overbeating, carefully fold the raspberry puree into the whipped cream mix.

2. In the rectangular serving dish, arrange the remaining fresh raspberries side by side to make a large red cross in the dish. Lay another layer of raspberries on top. Divide the raspberry fool into the four corners of the dish, taking care not to disturb the raspberry cross in the center. Using a spatula, smooth the fool until each of the four quarters is flat.

3. Place additional whipped cream in a piping bag with a star tube. Highlight the whole raspberry cross by piping small rosettes of cream along each sides of the cross.

MAKES 10 SERVINGS

Framboises St. George

LEMON CHEESE

Lemon cheese is not to be confused with lemon curd. Lemon curd is usually set with pectin or cornstarch and was the traditional filling, along with jam, for English scones. Lemon cheese uses more eggs and is much richer in flavor, as well as a lot thicker. Lemon cheese can be piped into tartlets, scones, and other pastry goods; lemon curd can't. I use organic eggs, as the feed often results in a creamier yellow yolk, which will in turn give me a lemon-colored cheese.

Microplanes have replaced old box graters in most cooks' kitchens. They produce a fine shaving of lemon zest that not only adds extra flavor, but also aids in the coloring. I've listed vanilla bean paste as one of the ingredients. It isn't as common as vanilla extract, but I've had good luck finding it at Whole Foods and other gourmet markets. Finally, the European-style butter (English butter if you can get it), with its creamier taste and silkier texture caused by the slower and longer churning, helps produce this velvety lemon cheese.

1/2 cup freshly squeezed lemon juice, about 3 lemons	2 teaspoons lemon zest
1/2 cup granulated sugar	1 pinch of salt
3 eggs	1 teaspoon vanilla paste
3 egg yolks	1 cup European unsalted butter, cut into small pieces

1. Set a large metal bowl over a saucepan of simmering water. Make sure the bowl doesn't touch the water. Add the lemon juice, sugar, eggs, yolks, zest, and salt. Whisk the ingredients together and keep stirring until the mixture starts to thicken. Keep moving the mixture with the whisk as it cooks on the bottom of the bowl.

2. Remove the mixture from the heat once it has thickened to the consistency of sour cream. Add the vanilla paste and butter. Whisk until combined. Cover with buttered parchment paper, and refrigerate for at least 24 hours before using. Refrigerated lemon cheese will keep for about one week.

MAKES ENOUGH TO SPREAD ON 16 SCONES
AND TO GIVE TO A FRIEND IN A JAR FOR EASTER

MULBERRY GIN

Sloe gin was one of the royal favorite tipples at shooting lunches and many of the guests would carry a hip flask filled with it. But then David Quick, one of my fellow chefs, and I started making mulberry gin with the ripe berries from the trees in Home Park. The purple color is amazing. Once the gin was decanted, the leftover berries could then be spooned into a casserole dish and topped with a little crumble mix and baked for a hearty winter pudding or even added to game stew. We had so many berries that I would double the recipe and make the mix in a wine store demijohn.

5	cups ripe mulberries	1	liter bottle gin
1¼	cups sugar	1	empty gin bottle

1. Wash the mulberries in cold water and pat dry with a paper towel. Prick each of the berries with a wooden toothpick several times to help release the juices. Put half the berries into the empty bottle and add half the sugar. Pour half the gin over the berries and place the cap on.

2. Add the remaining half of the mulberries and sugar to the now half-empty gin bottle. Replace the cap.

3. Shake both bottles several times to dissolve the sugar, and set them up in a cool, dark room for up to three months. Shake the bottles each day for the first week and then once a week after that. Decant the gin through a piece of cheesecloth into clean, sterilized bottles. The gin is ready to drink after one month, but is best after three months, and will keep for several years.

MAKES 2 LITERS

CHAPTER FOUR

HMY *Britannia*

Summer on the High Seas

For forty-four years the royal yacht *Britannia* served Queen Elizabeth II and her family. It took the royal family to 135 countries and on 968 official visits, steaming a total of 1,087,623 nautical miles. I—lucky chef—got to travel on some of those trips. In fact, during my years as a palace chef, I traveled to Australia and New Zealand, America, Malta, Sicily, Iceland, and France. And while I'll never be a hardy sailor—trust me on this—working on *Britannia* was an amazing introduction to people and places all over the globe.

HMY *Britannia* was a glorious vessel, able to accommodate nearly sixty guests for a royal dinner or as many as two hundred people for a "meet and greet" cocktail party. Stem to stern she measured more than 412 feet. The yacht was beautifully appointed with long sweeping staircases between levels; a grand formal dining room that hosted the rich, famous, and influential; and private suites used by honeymooning royals, including Princess Diana and Prince Charles.

I speak in the past tense because *Britannia* was decommissioned in 1997. By that time the yacht needed major retrofitting. The expense to do this was considerable, and the British government decided that the funds could better be used elsewhere. So, *Britannia* was sent to Edinburgh, Scotland, where she is now permanently anchored.

If Windsor Castle depicts all that is best about England, then *Britannia* put the "great" in Great Britain. The yacht would slowly glide into port with every sailor dressed up in pure white "number ones" and lined up side by side around the yacht, like a white ribbon around an immense gift. The Royal Marine Band, also in full uniform, would be playing on the top deck "Anchors Away" or "Rule *Britannia*." The entrance of *Britannia* into port was always an unabashed moment of pure spectacle and a royal reminder of British imperial glory. For all of us on deck, well, we stood a little taller and our heads were held high. We were proud to be British.

SUMMERTIME SAILING

At the beginning of August every year, *Britannia* sailed out of Portsmouth, heading toward the Isle of Wight for the annual Cowes Week racing regatta. Cowes Week yacht racing began in 1826, and today is the longest running and most pres-

An informal royal staff photo on Western Isles. I'm actually in the first row this time—very rare!

tigious international sailing regatta in the world. The event, which lasts eight days, takes place in the Solent waters off Cowes. This locale was picked for its sheltered waters and unusual tidal conditions that make it a challenging spot for even experienced racers. About one thousand yachts compete each year and the participating yacht clubs assemble their best teams of seasoned sailors who compete in these waters year after year. The Duke of Edinburgh loved competing in the races and I think that Cowes Week was his absolutely favorite time on board *Britannia*.

For the staff, Cowes Week was relatively easy. The Duke was often the only royal member of the family on board, and entertaining was primarily between the Duke and his friends, other avid yachtsmen. Tied to a buoy in the Solent, *Britannia* had one of the best views of the races, and the Duke and his guests were enthusiastic spectators when they weren't competing. The yacht was anchored so close to the action that on one occasion another yacht named *Scorcher* got entangled in *Britannia's* white flag, ripping it off altogether.

Her Majesty and the rest of the family would join *Britannia* later in

Southampton, and then the entire family would sail for ten days through the Western Isles of Scotland. The Western Isles are beautiful. A lush landscape dotted with grazing sheep and green, green, green. But all that green means lots of rain, and I'll admit that occasionally I would long for a bit of sunshine. Princess Diana felt the same way. I remember her commiserating with me one day on board *Britannia*.

Superman—with a little help!

"We always make a wrong turn on this trip, don't we Darren?" She asked me once. "We should be making a left out of Southampton and heading to the Mediterranean, not up to the Western Isles!"

I didn't hear any complaints from the rest of the family, though. The trip would be a leisurely zigzag from island to island, and the family would disembark for a picnic lunch or a hike about. Occasionally, while the royals were ashore, I'd watch the sailors fishing for mackerel, and if I was lucky, I'd persuade them to let me have a few to cook for the royal table. There were also fishermen who would pull up alongside the boat during the day, trying to sell a bit of their catch. It was really very peaceful. Meals were family affairs and there was very little official entertaining. Occasionally William and Harry would grow restless. I remember that once as a treat, a sailor dressed up as Superman and was tethered from a line of a helicopter flying overhead. The boys were convinced he was flying.

The highlight of the trip was visiting the Queen Mother at the Castle of Mey. The family would pull into Scrabster Harbor on a Sunday at lunchtime and head up to the castle for tea. In retrospect the small town of Thurso was quite remote, but after docking at nearly deserted islands for a week, Thurso felt quite continental with its one streetlight and pay phone! The family would rejoin the yacht in the evening. As we sailed out of Scrabster Harbor we would pass by the Queen Mum's castle. *Britannia*'s sailors would set off flares in front of the castle, and the castle staff would, in turn, set off fireworks to honor the passing ship. It was a lovely tribute from mother to daughter and made for a stunning nighttime sky.

SAILING ABROAD

On foreign trips, *Britannia* was the Queen's home away from home. Though Her Majesty might be on foreign turf, she would also use *Britannia* to give her guests a sense of Great Britain. So we didn't stray too far into local cuisine. I imagine, in fact, that some of our guests over the years thought the traditional British food we served was quite exotic! In order to replicate that English "feel," the provisions that stocked the yacht's larder were often packed and sent by the palace chefs before the trip.

For example, if the trip was to Australia, the dry provisions (coffee beans, sugar, tea, flour, Bendix bitter mints, Malvern water, etc.) would be loaded on board while the yacht was docked at Portsmouth as it readied to sail. For the next six weeks *Britannia* would wend her way down under and dock. Then the chefs would be flown from London to Australia, with hampers of all the perishable items and kitchen equipment we might need for Her Majesty's tour stowed on board.

Once abroad, all staff—whether on deck or on shore—represented Her Majesty and England. You were expected to be on best behavior and always properly attired. In fact, each staff member was fitted beforehand with a made-to-measure suit. If you weren't in chef whites, then you were expected to be in a suit—especially when embarking and disembarking *Britannia*. I'll admit it was a real pain having to shower and change into a suit just to pop ashore for a postcard.

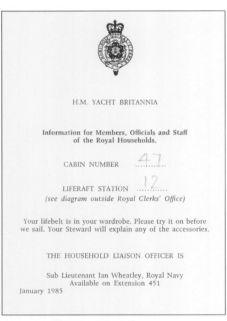

H.M. YACHT BRITANNIA

Information for Members, Officials and Staff of the Royal Households.

CABIN NUMBER 47

LIFERAFT STATION 12
(see diagram outside Royal Clerks' Office)

Your lifebelt is in your wardrobe. Please try it on before we sail. Your Steward will explain any of the accessories.

THE HOUSEHOLD LIAISON OFFICER IS

Sub Lieutenant Ian Wheatley, Royal Navy
Available on Extension 451
January 1985

Very important Britannia
safety information

Two especially memorable trips for me on *Britannia* were my very first trip in 1984 to France and a later trip to the United States in 1991. That first trip was a short one across the English Channel in June of 1984. Along with forty staff members, I hopped the train from London to Portsmouth. As I walked toward the yacht that first time, I was struck by its colors. *Britannia* had a dark blue hull with a red rudder sticking out of the water and a band of gold leaf encircling the top of the hull. I found out later that the Queen had chosen these colors to match Prince Philip's dragon-class racing yacht, *Bluebottle*.

I headed up the gangplank following the other four chefs through the galley kitchen and down to my cabin located right next to the propellers. Their insistent thumping would lull me to sleep at night whenever I sailed on *Britannia*. The room was compact with a tiny bed, a closet, and a writing desk. On the desk was a booklet informing me to head to life raft station 12 in the event that the yacht began to sink. Funny, I hadn't thought of that.

I started to feel slightly queasy and sat down for a moment on the bed, keenly aware of the slight rocking of the ship. Well, there was no way out now. I changed into my chef whites, grabbed my knife case, and headed back up to the kitchen. After wandering the ship for fifteen minutes, I conceded defeat and asked a passing sailor if he would be so kind as to take me to the royal galley. I was lost and embarrassed.

Of Mice and Men

In Tampa there was a rare free day when the Queen was being hosted at an onshore event. Several chef mates and I decided that a trip to Florida wasn't complete without a trip to Disney World. A chauffeured Lincoln Town Car was at our disposal, and properly suited up, we all piled in. As we approached Orlando, we asked our chauffeur to please pull into the nearest McDonald's.

We received plenty of stares as the black limo pulled into the parking lot and out stepped half a dozen men in finely cut suits all carrying small bags. Once inside McDonald's, we all ducked into the nearest restroom for a quick change into shorts and summer shirts. The suits just had to go! Now we were ready for a day with the big mouse and we jumped back into the limo—burgers in hand.

By the next morning the yacht had pulled into the city of Caen, and a crowd was gathered on Pegasus Bridge to greet us. We docked early and got busy preparing a lunch banquet for the king of Norway, the king of Belgium, the queen of the Netherlands, the Grand Duke of Luxembourg, and others. On the menu was Avocado *Britannia* (quite fitting), a tender braised stuffed chicken in a Champagne sauce, carrots and broccoli in hollandaise, and parsleyed jersey potatoes. For dessert

I made an ice cream soufflé with wild strawberries. It was a menu befitting our royal guests and a well-dealt response to our French critics who always said that the Brits couldn't cook!

Royal Gifts

I was always amazed by the gifts Her Majesty received. Some were lavish, like the gold figurine of a camel underneath two gold palm trees—a gift from the emir of Qatar. Some gifts were useful, like ties, scarves, and cufflinks; and some gifts were downright weird. In Florida, Her Majesty was presented with two sea cows to commemorate her visit. When we heard this, we chefs looked at each other in puzzlement. Were we expected to cook them? Fortunately they were just to be named by the Queen and then released back into the wild.

The Queen always gives a gift in return, and it is always the same—a signed photo of herself.

Later that day, *Britannia* weighed anchor and headed to Arrowmanches to take part in the fortieth anniversary of the landing at Normandy and then sailed back home. It had been a successful first trip for me. The banquet had gone well, I hadn't been seasick, and the yacht had stayed afloat. I never did find out where life raft station 12 was.

By the time I traveled to the United States in 1991 I was a seasoned chef on *Britannia*. That trip, however, marked my first time to America. The yacht docked in Miami for a week and then sailed on to Tampa. I'm not sure what I expected, but Florida took me completely by surprise. It was so tropical with lush vegetation everywhere. Warm breezes blew off the water and the night sky was a soft blue. Even though I was working hard, I felt completely relaxed and totally spoiled. I had flown from London on the *Concorde,* and now here I was with brilliantly clear waters beneath and sunshine overhead.

I remember that the trip was a big success for the Queen. There was a beautiful banquet for Presidents Ford and Reagan and their wives, Governor Lawton Chiles, future Governor Jeb Bush, Senators Bob Graham and Connie Mack, as well as a host of others. For that event we prepared Oeufs Drumkilbo, using the finest

Maine lobsters. That was followed with a saddle of lamb, which had been boned and stuffed with a chicken mousse and then garnished with asparagus tips and a Madeira sauce. I remember sending out a beautiful cold lemon soufflé as dessert.

After the banquet, the Queen hosted a formal cocktail party on deck for two hundred guests. That wasn't at all unusual, but it meant we chefs had to move quickly. So as soon as the royal dining table was cleared (including all twenty-four fruit bowls, which were dismantled and the remaining fruit stowed back down below) we turned our thoughts to canapés and food for the reception. Guests would arrive on board expecting lots to drink and eat while enjoying music performed by the Royal Marine Band. Appetizers had to be small, single-bite affairs, which could be swallowed quickly should a guest suddenly be introduced to a member of the royal family. Popular

Menu for Presidents Reagan and Ford

canapés were things like tartlets filled with finely chopped chicken in a mild curry sauce, smoked salmon roulades, or the ever-popular mini sausage roll.

Several years later when I was working for Princess Diana, we would have a recurring conversation about America. "Really, Darren," she would say, "we must go live there someday."

My reply was always the same. "Yes, your Royal Highness. I would like that." That trip to Florida had made a strong impact on me indeed!

IN THE GALLEY

It was amazing how much food five palace chefs could produce in *Britannia*'s tight kitchen quarters. There were two kitchens as part of the royal galley, one for pastry and the other, the main kitchen, for everything else. The pastry "kitchen" was really a pastry workspace since it had no oven. It was just a ten-foot-long galley with a small scuttle hole that let you look outside onto the sea.

The main kitchen was about twice as big as the pastry kitchen and included a scullery area, a vegetable prep area, and the main cooking space. In the center of the galley was a square stainless steel table that four chefs worked around. It had lips on the end to stop any dishes from sliding off. Behind that worktable were two stoves with two ovens underneath, and off to the side were two convection ovens, primarily for pastry and always kept at 350 degrees. Two broilers, two small

Beat Retreat

At a cocktail reception, the Royal Marine Band always finishes the evening with a drum cadence to "beat retreat." This military tradition dates back to the 1500s when Britain was often engaged in wars against its European neighbors. It was agreed by both warring parties that as soon as it got dark, fighting would end. So drums would beat a cadence at dusk to signal troops to halt fighting and "retreat" back to camp.

Through the years, this drumming tradition became associated with the lowering of the British flag each evening. On *Britannia*, all guests would stand on the two upper decks and look out on the floodlit mast. The Royal Marine Band would march back and forth on the quay side until the flag was lowered. Once done, guests knew the party had come to an end and it was time to disembark.

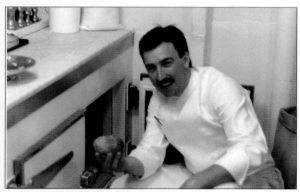

In the pastry kitchen, laughing at the "bullet hard" mangoes they had sent me for royal dinner

refrigerators, and a bain marie made up the rest of the galley. Not much equipment for a floating palace kitchen, but we made it work.

Oddly enough, the main storage fridge was located three decks below, shared with the yacht's other two galleys. Need more tomatoes? You would have to contact the dedicated sailor assistant, with the rank of "leading hand," to go down and bring it up for you. Want to take a look at the pears and make sure they will be ripe for tomorrow's banquet? The leading hand would have to negotiate three flights of stairs to fetch them for you and the same again to take them back—regardless of how calm or rough the sea might be.

Now when I say three flights down, it wasn't via the ship's staircases. The actual route from one floor to another on the working part of the yacht was via ladders. On *Britannia* you climbed up and down ladders all the time. But it was a little tricky to climb when you also had your hands full with a tray of chocolate mousse. The leading hand would balance food boxes and trays on his shoulders and climb up and down the ladders balancing his load as best he could.

Occasionally a tip in the swelling seas would result in a box flying off his shoulders and back down onto the floor. More than once I would get a box of really bruised fruit, but I didn't dare complain. Being the leading hand was a bru-

Waves Outside and Inside

I loved *Britannia* most when we were docked! I'm a chef, not a sailor, and I've never been able to handle sailing in bad weather. Once after a successful state visit to Australia we set sail for New Zealand and headed out to the Bass Strait, a body of water notorious for its rough swells. Cheese soufflé was on the menu that night for dinner instead of something easy like cold pudding.

As I was cooking, the Queen's page kept coming through the galley and announcing that the head count for dinner was dropping. By this time I'd broken out in a sweat and my hands were clammy, but I was determined to see the soufflés finished before heading down to my cabin. Just to check, I opened the oven and saw the soufflés wobbling back and forth in their silver dishes, in tempo with the yacht's sway. That did it. Everything in the room started to wobble. I was able to serve the soufflés, but shortly thereafter I joined the others who couldn't stomach the seas.

tal job and that sailor had all my sympathy. Unfortunately, I wasn't able to fetch them myself. Civilians, "civvies" as the "yachtees" affectionately called us, were banned from going below decks and carrying food up. It was deemed unsafe.

There was a certain rhythm to cooking on *Britannia*. As soon as you boarded you checked all your provisions to make sure nothing had been lost between the palace and the yacht. Chefs traveled with their own knives and chef whites for just that reason. After that you started getting tea ready. The timing was tight. If the chefs were on board, that meant in a few hours the Queen and the rest of the royal entourage would be boarding.

So you finished prepping for tea (the tea cakes had already been made and transported) and you immediately began setting up fruit bowls, which would be sent to all the royal staterooms. Tins of fresh leaves would have been packed alongside the food, and we used those as decoration. There wouldn't be any more once we were out at sea. When that was done, we put up gallons of lemon refresher. Lemon refresher is a kind of early lemonade with the unusual addition of Epsom salts.

Civvies at work in the royal galley

Since Epsom salt is also a slight natural laxative, we always had to be right on when measuring out this recipe! The family loved it and we always made up a big batch once on board. We would also take out the butter pats and make hundreds of tiny butter balls which could be frozen ahead and used on bread plates for dinner. Some chefs would be making quarts of salad dressing, either French vinaigrette or a creamy chive dressing. Salad was always served at mealtimes, and making lots of dressing in advance saved time.

I would fall into the routine after a few days. It always took me a little while to get my sea legs and to figure out how to work the tight quarters. Also, I had to adjust my cooking to take into account weather conditions. Cooking in warmer climates could be difficult. If the weather was hot and muggy, icings and gelatins wouldn't set and refrigeration wasn't close by. Sometimes I'd sneak a cake into the air-conditioned dining room just to cool the frosting down to the right temperature.

FRENCH DRESSING

The Queen's favorite and the only one requested dressing when dining alone.

1 cup corn oil	1 teaspoon finely chopped fresh tarragon
1/3 cup white wine vinegar	
1 teaspoon Dijon mustard	Salt and freshly ground pepper

In a large bowl whisk the oil, vinegar, and mustard together. Add the tarragon and salt and pepper to taste.

MAKES 1 1/2 CUPS

BEEF CARBONNADE

4 tablespoons vegetable oil, divided	3 tablespoons all-purpose flour
2 pounds lean stewing beef, cut into 2-inch cubes	1 1/4 cups beef broth
	1 1/4 cups Newcastle brown ale
1 large onion, peeled and sliced	1 bay leaf
3 cloves garlic, chopped	1/2 teaspoon dried thyme
3 large carrots, peeled and chopped	1/2 teaspoon salt
4 ribs celery, chopped	4 ounces button mushrooms, quartered

1. Preheat the oven to 350 degrees. Heat 2 tablespoons oil in a large, covered casserole, and brown the meat. When the meat is brown, set it aside in a bowl. In the same casserole, add the remaining 2 tablespoons oil, and sauté the onions, garlic, carrots, and celery. Return the meat to the casserole and add the flour. Cook for 1 minute, stirring constantly. Stir in the broth and brown ale, and add the bay leaf, thyme, salt, and mushrooms.

2. Bring the meat mixture to a boil, cover, and place the casserole in the center of the oven for 1 1/2 to 2 hours, or until the meat is tender. Remove the bay leaf before serving. Serve with mashed potatoes.

MAKES 4 SERVINGS

EGGS DRUMKILBO

This dish was the Queen Mother's favorite and one we always put on the menu when she came to stay. It was also served at the wedding breakfast of Princess Anne and Captain Mark Phillips in 1973.

2	(1½-pound) lobsters, cooked and cooled		1	teaspoon Worcestershire sauce
8	hard-boiled eggs, divided		1	packet unflavored gelatin
6	vine-ripe tomatoes		1	cup sherry
2	cups mayonnaise		6	medium shrimp
½	cup ketchup		6	parsley sprigs for garnish
				Salt and freshly ground pepper

1. Remove the meat from the lobster tails and claws, and dice into bite-size pieces. Dice 6 eggs into the same size pieces as the lobster.

2. Bring 4 cups water to a rolling boil in a heavy-bottomed pan. Cut out the green stem portion of the tomatoes and drop them into the boiling water for about 30 seconds. Remove immediately to ice cold water, and leave for several minutes. Peel the skins off the tomatoes, and dry the tomatoes with paper towels. Cut the tomatoes into quarters, and remove the seeds and membranes. Dice the tomato flesh into the same size pieces as the egg and lobster.

3. In a large ceramic or glass bowl (not metallic), whisk the mayonnaise, ketchup, and Worcestershire sauce together until combined. Add the lobster, egg, and tomato, and fold together gently. Taste and season with salt and pepper. Spoon the egg and lobster mixture into an ornate glass dish, and smooth the top to make it level.

4. Soften the gelatin with the sherry in a small pan. Place over a low heat, and stir until dissolved. Spoon a thin layer of the sherry over the top of the egg and lobster mixture and refrigerate the dish until the layer has set.

5. Using an egg slicer, cut six circles of egg from the remaining two eggs. Brush the tops of each egg slice with some of the remaining warm gelatin. Cut each of the shrimp in half lengthwise, dip into the gelatin, and arrange neatly on an egg slice. Refrigerate until set, and then lift each egg and shrimp garnish to decorate the egg and lobster salad. Garnish each with 1 sprig of parsley. Serve as an appetizer with lemon wedges and sliced and buttered brown bread.

MAKES 6 SERVINGS.

CHEESE SOUFFLÉ

The Queen often requested this soufflé. She would drive a spoon straight down the middle and pour fresh cream right in.

1 tablespoon unsalted butter, for greasing	1½ teaspoons potato starch
1¼ cups heavy cream plus 1 cup for garnish	6 tablespoons freshly grated Parmesan cheese
1½ tablespoons all-purpose flour	1 teaspoon butter
⅛ teaspoon cayenne pepper	6 eggs, separated
	Salt and freshly ground pepper

1. Preheat oven to 400 degrees. Place a baking sheet in the center of the oven.

2. Liberally grease the sides and bottom of an 8-inch soufflé dish with the unsalted butter, and spread a thick layer (about ⅛ inch thick) around the top edge of the dish. This will ensure that the soufflé rises above the top. Refrigerate.

3. In a heavy saucepan, add the cream, flour, cayenne, potato starch, Parmesan, and 1 teaspoon butter over a high heat, and whisk until the butter melts and the mixture comes together into a thick sauce. Remove from the heat and whisk in the egg yolks. Season with salt and pepper to taste, and allow the mixture to cool for about 10 minutes.

4. Whip the egg whites until stiff and fold them into the cheese mixture until the egg whites and cheese mixture are combined. Spoon into the prepared soufflé dish, and place the soufflé on top of the baking sheet. Bake for 18 minutes, or until the top is golden brown. Remove from the oven, and serve straightaway with a jug of heavy cream.

MAKES 6 SERVINGS

Cheese Soufflé

POJARSKI SMITANE

Pojarski

4	slices white bread, crusts removed, cut into a 1/4-inch dice
1	cup buttermilk
1	pound ground veal
1	lemon, zest only
3	cloves garlic, crushed
1/2	cup grated Parmesan cheese
1/2	cup finely diced red bell peppers
1/2	cup finely diced celery
1/4	teaspoon celery seeds
1/4	cup finely chopped fresh dill
1/4	cup finely chopped green onion
	Salt and freshly ground pepper

Sauce

1/2	stick (1/4 cup) butter
1	cup finely diced onion
1/2	cup white wine
2	tablespoons all-purpose flour
1	tablespoon paprika
1	cup beef broth
1/2	cup heavy cream
1	tablespoon lemon juice
	Salt and freshly ground pepper
1/4	cup vegetable oil, for frying
1/2	cup sour cream
1/4	cup finely chopped fresh dill

1. **For the pojarski,** place the bread into a small bowl with the buttermilk to soak for at least 10 minutes. Combine the veal, lemon zest, garlic, Parmesan, peppers, celery, celery seeds, dill, green onions, and salt and pepper to taste in a large bowl and mix well. Add the bread and buttermilk, and mix again. Shape the mix into teardrops about 3 inches long, 2 inches wide at the widest point, and 1 1/4 inch high. Place on a greased tray and refrigerate.

2. **For the sauce,** melt the butter in a heavy saucepan over a high heat. Stir in the onions, reduce the heat, and cook until soft and translucent. Add the wine and bring the mixture to a boil. Cook for several minutes, and then remove from the heat and stir in the flour and paprika. Add the beef broth and cream and reduce to a saucelike consistency. Add the lemon juice, and season with the salt and pepper. Set aside and keep warm.

3. Place a large frying pan over a high heat, and add the vegetable oil. Cook the pojarski in batches so not to crowd the pan. Cook for about 3 minutes per side.

4. Pour the sauce into the bottom of a large serving dish. Arrange the pojarski neatly around the edge. Swirl the sour cream in the center of the dish, and sprinkle with the chopped dill.

MAKES 6 SERVINGS

Pojarski Smitane

TENDERLOIN STEAKS WITH STILTON AND WALNUT CRUST AND MUSHROOM CREAM SAUCE

Mushroom sauce

2	tablespoons unsalted butter
1	small onion, finely chopped
1	clove garlic, crushed
12	ounces (2 cups) Baby Bella or cremini mushrooms, sliced
	Pinch of salt
2	tablespoons all-purpose flour
1	cup homemade or canned beef broth
1/2	cup heavy cream
	Salt and freshly ground pepper

Steaks

4	center-cut beef tenderloin steaks, about 6 ounces each
	Salt and pepper
1	tablespoon olive oil
4	ounces crumbled Stilton cheese
1/4	cup chopped walnuts
1	tablespoon finely chopped fresh parsley

1. Preheat the oven to 400 degrees.

2. **For the sauce,** melt the butter in a large sauté pan, and add the onions, garlic, mushrooms, and a pinch of salt. Sauté the vegetables until they start to soften. Stir in the flour and let cook in the butter for a minute. Add the beef broth and keep stirring until the sauce thickens. Add the cream and reduce slightly.

3. Remove the pan from the heat, and using a hand blender, blend the sauce. Once blended, return the pan to the heat. Adjust the consistency, and thin the sauce down with a little cream if it appears too thick. Season with salt and pepper to taste. Keep the sauce warm until the steaks are cooked. The sauce can be made up to a day ahead at this point and refrigerated. Just warm the sauce over a low flame.

4. **For the steaks**, let them come to room temperature. Season to taste with salt and pepper. In a separate sauté pan large enough to hold the steaks in one layer, add the olive oil and heat until hot but not smoking. Add the steaks and cook for about 2 minutes on each side. Remove the pan from the heat, top each steak with some of the Stilton and walnuts, and place the pan in the hot oven for 10 minutes, or until done.

5. Remove the pan from the oven, and transfer the steaks to a clean plate. Let them rest for at least 5 minutes. Check the sauce and warm if needed. Serve the steaks on a bed of the sauce, and garnish with finely chopped parsley over each steak.

MAKES 4 SERVINGS.

HADDOCK ST. GERMAIN

Britain is famous for its fish and chips, and although I never saw the royal family eat them the traditional way, out of a newspaper, this is about as close as they came. The fish can be prepared—ready to broil—several hours in advance.

2 large russet potatoes	2 egg yolks
4 cups vegetable oil, for deep frying	4 (6-ounce) haddock fillets, preferably center cut
1½ cups Japanese panko bread crumbs, or regular bread crumbs	Kosher salt and ground white pepper
¼ cup all-purpose flour	¼ cup finely chopped chives
1 stick (8 tablespoons) unsalted butter	

1. Preheat the broiler to high. Peel the potatoes and shape them into rectangles. Cut the potatoes into 1½ x ¼ x ¼-inch pieces and immerse them in cold water. Heat the oil to 250 degrees. Drain the potatoes and pat them dry with a paper towel. Place the potatoes into the hot oil, and cook until the potatoes are soft but not colored. Lift out onto a tray lined with paper towels, and allow the potatoes to cool. Set aside the frying oil for use later.

2. Spread the panko crumbs onto a dinner plate. Do the same with the flour on a separate plate. Melt the butter and stir in the egg yolks. Coat each of the haddock fillets first in the flour, then the egg and butter mix, and finally the panko. Make sure the fish is completely coated, and then place each piece onto a baking sheet about 1 inch apart. Season with salt and pepper to taste. Broil the haddock for about 8 minutes until the panko coating is golden brown and the fish is tender.

3. While the fish is broiling, reheat the oil to 375 degrees. Carefully drop the potatoes in the oil, and cook for about 5 minutes until golden and crispy. Remove to a plate and use a paper towel to drain off the excess oil. Season with salt.

4. Lift the haddock off the baking sheet onto the serving plates, and add the crispy golden potatoes. Garnish with the chives and serve with hollandaise sauce, if desired.

MAKES 4 SERVINGS

LEMON REFRESHER

One of the first jobs after boarding Britannia *was to make lemon refresher. Every member of the royal family would reach for a refreshing glass of this English "homemade lemonade" while sitting on deck. This calls for a few special ingredients you might not have in the cupboard. The Epsom salts you can find at Whole Foods, and the citric acid and tartaric acid are common ingredients in beer making. You can find them at beer-making supply stores or through online sources.*

4½	cups sugar	3	teaspoons tartaric acid
2	tablespoons Epsom salts	6	lemons, juice and zest
3	teaspoons citric acid	5	cups water

Place the sugar, Epsom salts, citric acid, tartaric acid, lemon juice, and zest in a bowl and whisk them together. Bring the 5 cups water to a boil and pour it over the lemon mix, whisking until combined. Refrigerate until cold and decant into screw-top bottles. To serve, dilute ¼ cup of the lemon refresher with 2 cups of water over ice or to taste.

MAKES 2 QUARTS CONCENTRATE

COLD LEMON SOUFFLÉ

3	lemons, juice and zest	1¼	cups heavy cream, whipped until stiff
3	eggs, separated	1½	cups heavy cream, whipped stiff for rosette garnish
¾	cup sugar		Grated chocolate
1	packet unflavored gelatin		
5	tablespoons water		

1. Fold a sheet of parchment paper in half, and then wrap it around the outside of an 8-inch soufflé dish. It should extend three inches higher than the lip. Staple the top and bottom of the parchment tightly. Place the parchment-wrapped soufflé dish on a baking sheet, and place the baking sheet in the refrigerator to chill.

2. Place the lemon juice, zest, egg yolks, and sugar in a large mixing bowl that will fit snugly on a pan of boiling water, and whisk the ingredients until combined. Heat for

Cold Lemon Soufflé

about 2 minutes until the mixture heats up, whisking occasionally. Remove from the heat, and whisk with an electric mixer until the mixture is cool. Meanwhile, soften the gelatin in the water, and warm it just to dissolve. Add the gelatin to the egg mixture, and whisk it in.

3. In a large bowl whip the egg whites until stiff. Fold them into the egg yolk mixture, alternating with 1¼ cups whipped cream. Remove the baking sheet from the refrigerator, and carefully pour the filling into the soufflé dish, making sure that it comes at least 1 inch above the lip of the dish and is touching the parchment. Don't touch the soufflé dish or parchment, but instead use the baking sheet to move the soufflé into the refrigerator. Refrigerate 6 to 8 hours or overnight. Carefully peel off the parchment paper and discard.

4. Garnish the top of the soufflé with rosettes of whipped cream, and sprinkle the chocolate on top.

MAKES 6 SERVINGS

TARTE TATIN

The Tatin sisters in France invented this dish more than one hundred years ago. Not long after that it made its way to the palace and became a royal favorite. The dish is still served all across France, usually with a big bowl of crème fraiche. The royal family prefers it with a bowl of crème chantilly flavored with brandy—a lot of it.

If you can't find lard, then shortening is a reasonable substitute. You can also make this using just European butter; it's a lot richer and crumblier, but delicious.

Pastry

1¼ cups all-purpose flour
¼ teaspoon salt
1½ sticks (¾ cup) chilled unsalted butter
¼ cup lard or shortening
    Cold water

Caramel

2 cups sugar
1½ cups water, divided

Filling

½ stick (¼ cup) unsalted butter
2 pounds Granny Smith apples, peeled and sliced
1 lemon, zested and juiced
¼ cup granulated sugar

1. **For the pastry**, pulse the flour and salt a few times in a food processor fitted with a metal blade, just to mix. Cut the chilled butter and lard into cubes, and add it to the flour mixture. Pulse briefly until the mixture forms little balls, like moist crumbs, with no chunks of butter or lard visible. Remember, you have to pulse, not run, the food processor.

2. Sprinkle 1 tablespoon cold water over the surface of the dough. Pulse once. Repeat with 2 to 3 more tablespoons and pulse briefly. Add more water if needed, 1 tablespoon at a time. The dough should be slightly sticky, but stiff enough to come together to form a ball. Wrap the dough in plastic. Form it into a flattened ball, and refrigerate for at least 30 minutes.

3. Preheat the oven to 350 degrees.

4. **For the caramel**, bring the sugar and water to a boil in a small, heavy-bottomed saucepan. Once the mixture comes to a boil, whisk gently, and then let it boil without stirring until the sugar is a golden caramel color. Working quickly, pour about one-third

of the caramel into the bottom of a lightly greased 9-inch cake pan, swirling the pan to get the caramel to cover the whole bottom. Set the cake pan aside.

5. Carefully add about ½ cup water to the remaining caramel in the saucepan, and let it cool.

6. **For the filling**, melt the butter in a skillet large enough to hold all the apples. Add the sugar, apples, lemon zest, and juice. Cook for 5 minutes, or until the apples start to soften. Remove from the heat, and allow the apples to cool, tilting the skillet so that the juices run off the apples. Arrange a portion of apple pieces in a decorative fashion on the bottom of the caramelized cake pan until the apples fill one layer. Then top with all the remaining apples.

7. Roll out the pastry dough to about ½ inch thick, and place the dough over the top of the apples, cutting around the edges of the cake pan to fit.

8. Place in the oven for 20 to 30 minutes, or until the caramel starts to bubble around the edges of the crust. Remove from the oven, and carefully invert the pan onto a warm plate. Pour the remaining caramel sauce over the top of the apples, and serve with whipped cream laced with brandy.

MAKES 6 SERVINGS

YOGURT BRÛLÉE WITH MANGO AND PAPAYA

1¼	cups heavy whipping cream	1	ripe mango
1	500-gram container (about 2 cups) Total Greek yogurt	1	small papaya
½	cup Demerara sugar	1	lime, zested and juiced

1. In a large bowl whip the cream until stiff. Fold in the yogurt, and spoon into a serving dish. Sprinkle the Demerara sugar over the top, and refrigerate for at least 24 hours. The sugar crystallizes and forms a crispy topping.

2. Peel and dice the mango and papaya into a small bowl. Stir the lime zest and juice into the fruit mix. Serve the fruit alongside the brûlée.

MAKES 4 SERVINGS

JAM AND CREAM SPONGE

This is a versatile recipe. The cake is a light genoise, which we sometimes split in half and filled with a honey or lemon flavored cheese. But more often we would fill it with whipped cream and homemade strawberry jam made from the Queen's strawberries grown at Balmoral Castle.

2	tablespoons unsalted butter, for greasing
6	egg yolks
2	eggs
1/2	cup plus 1 tablespoon sugar
1/2	teaspoon vanilla paste

1/2	cup plus 2 tablespoons all-purpose flour
1/2	stick (1/4 cup) unsalted butter, melted
1	cup raspberry seedless jam
2	cups heavy cream, whipped stiff
1	tablespoon powdered sugar

1. Preheat the oven to 350 degrees. Lightly grease an 8 x 3-inch cake ring, and place a circle of parchment paper on the base. Grease the parchment paper.

2. Set a large mixing bowl over a pan of boiling water, and add the yolks, eggs, sugar, and vanilla paste to the bowl. (The bowl should be touching the water.) Whisk together until the mixture is combined. Whisk occasionally until the egg mixture starts to get hot. Remove the mixing bowl from the heat, and whisk with an electric mixer until the bowl becomes cold and the egg mixture has doubled in volume and is pale in color.

3. Sift the flour and add it to the egg mixture along with the melted butter, folding it in carefully by hand. Pour the mix into the prepared cake ring and bake for 20 minutes in the center of the oven, or until the top is golden brown and springs back when lightly pressed.

4. Remove the cake sponge from the oven and invert it onto a cooling rack. Leave the sponge on the rack until it is cold. Remove the cake ring and parchment paper carefully, and slice the sponge into three horizontal layers. Spread the raspberry jam equally on the bottom two layers. Top these bottom two layers equally with the whipped cream. Place the middle layer carefully on top of the bottom layer. Finish by placing the top layer on the middle layer. Dust with the powdered sugar and serve.

MAKES 8 SERVINGS

ISLE OF WIGHT PUDDING

This pudding is an old British dish that used to contain currants and raisins and was drizzled with golden syrup. Milk was poured over the pastry to make a syrupy sauce. Changing the filling to blueberries and drizzling with honey makes this dish taste delicious. Pouring cream on top, instead of milk, creates a lavender syrup sauce that looks heavenly too.

2	cups all-purpose flour	2	cups blueberries
1/2	cup lard or vegetable shortening	3/4	cup honey
1	stick (8 tablespoons) unsalted butter	1/2	cup heavy cream
1	teaspoon vanilla paste	1	tablespoon granulated sugar
2	tablespoons water		

1. In a large bowl combine the flour, lard, butter, and vanilla paste, and rub them together with your fingers until the mixture resembles fine crumbs. Then gradually stir in the water until it forms a crumbly dough. Wrap the dough in plastic wrap, and chill for about one hour. While the dough is resting, preheat the oven to 350 degrees, and set a rack on the middle shelf.

2. On a lightly floured surface, using a lightly floured rolling pin, roll the dough into a 12 x 8-inch rectangle, keeping the dough's thickness at about 1/2 inch. Cover the dough with the blueberries and drizzle the honey over the top.

3. With the short side of the rectangle facing you, roll up the dough, and place it on a jelly roll pan, seam side on the bottom. Crumple up some sheets of aluminum foil to pack around the sides of the roll to support it as it bakes. Bake in the middle of the oven for about 20 minutes. The pastry should be a golden brown, and the berries should burst, oozing their juices.

4. Remove the pan from the oven, take away the aluminum foil, and carefully pour the cream over the top of the roll. Sprinkle the granulated sugar over the roll, and return it to the oven for another 15 minutes. Remove the pan from the oven and spoon the syrup in the bottom of the pan over the top of the roll. Allow to cool for at least 15 minutes before slicing. Slice the roll on the baking sheet, and transfer each slice to a serving dish or plate. Serve with clotted cream or whipped cream.

MAKES 6 SERVINGS

CHAPTER FIVE

Balmoral Castle

Autumn in the Highlands

Balmoral Castle is the holiday home of the royal family. They vacation here each year beginning in late August and stay through early October. The castle, located in Scotland, just fifty miles west of Aberdeen, covers more than fifty thousand acres of land. The river Dee, which flows next to the castle, is loaded with fish, especially salmon, and there is plenty of game for the catching. It is a beautiful, somewhat wild location and as private a place as the royal family could hope to find.

My first trip to Balmoral Castle came two weeks after I had started working. I was sent up on the overnight train from London for staff "changeover day." Along with about one hundred other members of the Buckingham Palace staff, I boarded the overnight sleeper at Kings Cross station in London, bound for Aberdeen. Once in Scotland, we boarded a chartered coach going into the highlands along the A93 to the castle.

Before me was this huge castle I had heard so much about. I remember the coffee room maid Anne Gardner pointing out Lochnagar, a thirty-eight-hundred-foot black mountain peak, in the distance. "The Queen calls it her mountain jewel," the maid said with pride. Indeed.

As the coach turned into the outer edge of the property, we passed the old Crathie Kirk—the church where the royal family would attend religious services—went across the river, and continued through the main gate. I was extremely excited, as well as quite nervous, because I would now be cooking for the royal family, instead of feeding staff at Buckingham Palace. The coach turned up the chain walk and came to a halt at the Penn door—in effect, the back door to the castle. We disembarked and I was directed to lodgings over the garage. I dumped my bags on the bed, quickly changed into chef's whites, and headed to the castle kitchen. Outside on the walkway it hit me—the deep silence of the place and the smell of more than ten thousand acres of pine trees.

Looking up to the Penn door, the Balmoral staff entrance. If you look through the arch and into the Penn yard, you can see the kitchen windows.

Balmoral is a working castle, employing fifty full-time staff and as many as one hundred part-timers when the royal family is in residence. Castle employees farm three hundred acres, and seventy-five acres are rented out to neighboring farms. Prince Philip, the Queen's husband, has improved the grounds, building a formal garden, water garden, and most importantly—for the chefs—a kitchen garden. Mr. John Young oversees all the gardens. His team works all year long to ensure that the gardens look their best come summer. The kitchen garden was a joy for me. I especially loved the raspberries grown there. They were so full of juice that after picking a bucket, your hands and your chef's whites were stained pink. The taste was incomparable—and I know, because only one of every two berries picked ever made it into my bucket.

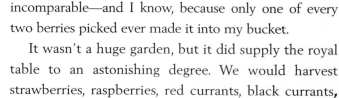

In the larder kitchen

It wasn't a huge garden, but it did supply the royal table to an astonishing degree. We would harvest strawberries, raspberries, red currants, black currants, gooseberries, frais de bois, blackberries, tayberries, rhubarb, and, of course, blueberries. Then there were the plums. The variety planted was called the Victoria plum, and to this day I've never tasted any finer. The trees were prolific producers, so everyone got their share. Princess Diana adored them, and the Duke would tuck a few in his pocket after a visit to the pastry kitchen.

The vegetables were just what you'd expect from an English garden. Plenty of onions, carrots, cabbage, potatoes, spring onions, turnips, leeks, English peas, and lettuces were grown there. And in a nod to more modern tastes, there were also all kinds of squash, beets, beans, cauliflower, and celeriac. We used it all—and if the year brought a good harvest, then the staff got spoiled too.

SHOOTING PARTIES

Shooting parties take place nearly every weekend at Balmoral. Guests arrive Friday evening in time for dinner and some serious planning for the next day's shoot. Gentlemen guests, who still make up the majority of shooters, are up early for breakfast the next day. A typical buffet breakfast would be fishcakes with fresh tomato sauce, poached eggs en croûte, deviled kidneys, and Curried Salmon Kedgeree. It is hearty food meant to last you until lunchtime.

Ladies join the men later. Some intrepid female guests might collect felled birds and pass them on to the ghillies, or gamekeepers, to tag and send to the game larder. Each guest receives a brace of birds as their parting weekend gift. The remaining birds are sent to the kitchen.

Shooting day lunches are alfresco affairs and a step back in time. Lunch is loaded onto silver trays with lids, which we called "hot boxes," and three trays can fit into a leather case. These cases are beautiful antiques, dating back to the reign

Wild Balmoral

Balmoral Castle is abutted by at least one thousand acres of dense forest. The royal family has worked hard to reestablish what was once a severely depleted deer population. The pine forest provides sanctuary for red and roe deer, red and black grouse, squirrels, golden eagles, and osprey. Generally hunting, which in England is called "stalking," happens during the early part of the week and shooting is done on Thursday, Friday, and Saturday. Deer hunting at Balmoral helps manage the red deer herd, protects the local habitat, and ensures the long-term health of the wild deer population.

The estate also keeps animals, including some rare breeds. One of the most unusual is an extremely old sheep breed called Soay. In appearance, they look like small woolly deer. The meat from these animals is sweet, very lean, and similar in taste to elk. It is the Kobe beef of lamb.

of King George VI. They were crafted out of the finest wood, lined with padding, and finished with red leather. It's a regal presentation for an outdoor lunch.

William and Harry, the youngest royals, were too young to either shoot or hunt deer. But they didn't want to miss out entirely. So they would often go out after tea in a Land Rover to hunt rabbits. It was considered good practice for both boys and it served a practical purpose. The rabbits were cleaned, cooked, deboned, and chopped for the Queen's corgis' dinner.

With all the shooting and hunting going on, it was no wonder we had game on the menu most days at Balmoral. The Duke would have us marinate the finer cuts, the loins and fillets, and then he would barbecue them in the evening. Second class joints would be cut up for stews, braised in red wine, and served with mashed potatoes during the next shooting lunch. Third class joints would be sent to the butcher in the village to grind up for sausages, and also later barbecued.

THE BOUNTIFUL RIVER DEE

Balmoral is a fisherman's paradise as well. The River Dee is one of the four major salmon running rivers in Great Britain, and it is a fast flowing river that winds its way toward the next closest town, Ballater. As it flows downward, the river eddies into pools here and there, perfect spots for salmon, grilse, and sea

The Huntress Diana

Princess Diana wasn't keen on hunting, shooting, or fishing. "Why does everyone in this family like killing things?" she asked me one day in the pastry kitchen. She was chafing at the pressure put on her by Prince Charles and other family members to hunt a stag. One day she went out early with her favorite ghillie, Sandy Masson. She was gone most of the day, but was in the kitchen when I returned to cook dinner that evening.

"I did it!" she yelled. "I got one, I shot a deer . . . poor thing." You could tell she was happy and sad at the same time.

"Darren, do me a favor," she asked. "Tell me when it will be served for dinner. I just can't do it. I can't bear the thought of that deer looking up at me from my plate."

trout to rest. Grilse are young salmon, usually four-year-olds, making their first journey upstream to spawn. There was just such a spot in the river not five minutes from the castle kitchen and it was a favorite of Princes William and Harry. They launched paddleboats from a small sandy bank near the river and would play there for hours. They also learned to fish at an early age from their dad.

Prince Charles is an avid fisherman and would spend hours standing in the Dee, often alongside the Queen Mother with water up to the tops of their waders. He would heft enormous salmon into the royal kitchen to be weighed, tagged, and catalogued. This was salmon so fresh its eyes seemed to follow you around the room. None of the chefs were allowed to touch it until instructions were sent from upstairs. Usually it would be grilled, poached, or broiled with a garnish and served on silver in the dining room. The trimmings weren't wasted either—goujons de saumon with sauce Tyrolienne always brought a smile in the royal nursery at high tea.

A FAMILY ON HOLIDAY

At Balmoral I saw the royal family up close, something nearly impossible at Buckingham Palace. For them it was vacation and the mood was relaxed. Most of the family would come down to the kitchen at some point. If we didn't see them in the kitchen, then we would see them at the Ghillies Ball and maybe even have a dance or two.

Balmoral welcomed the extended royal family as well. One charming guest was Lady Sarah Armstrong Jones, the Queen's niece, who visited each summer on holiday from university. She was a kind young lady with a sweet tooth. Shortbread was her favorite. We made sure to pack a tin or two in her luggage before she left in the fall.

Even though I was working, Balmoral always felt like a holiday to me. I don't think I was alone in that feeling. Whether true or anecdotal, there seemed to be an increase in staff liaisons at Balmoral. It was given the nickname "immoral Balmoral."

Dress was extremely casual. I entered the kitchens one morning and saw an older gentleman standing around in a frayed sweater with holes in the elbows. The pants had seen better days too, and the boots were muddy. I didn't pay much attention. He was just a gardener, probably looking for something to eat.

Prince Andrew being welcomed by the royal staff after returning from the Falklands. Prince Charles was there, too, dressed as the old man of Lochnagar.

In passing I asked a fellow chef the gardener's name. "Gardener?" he laughed. "You mean the Duke?" It was Prince Philip, the Queen's husband, and I hadn't recognized him.

I'm afraid that for Princess Diana, Balmoral was a bit of a trial. That spirit of "tromp around in your old Barbour and wellies" was not exactly her style. She was an elegant clotheshorse. Old rubber boots were the last thing you were apt to find in her closet. So, while the rest of the family was outfitted with waders for salmon fishing, Diana could be found with the boys, William and Harry, in the nursery. She would come down to the kitchen midmorning, often with William and Harry in full riding gear, for orange juice or cereal. Then they would all trek off to the stables for the boys' riding lessons. William rode a small pony named Smokey and the princess would walk alongside. Other times all three would pop in for snacks, usually fruit, before heading off to the boat pool to splash in the Dee. Prince Charles was rarely with them, preferring to hunt or paint pictures at his easel.

Late evening meals drove the princess a bit crazy as well. Dinner at Balmoral didn't usually begin until eight fifteen, or later if the Duke decided to barbecue up in the hills. Then everything was loaded onto a trailer and transported to the site. It wasn't unusual for dinner to finish around eleven. The Duke loved grilling out-

The lodge's dining room

doors and other family members would pitch in as well. Unfortunately, they wouldn't let Princess Diana anywhere near the grill. Her job, along with the Queen's, was to pull on yellow rubber gloves and rinse the pots in the sink afterward. Indeed, it was not her favorite way to pass the evening.

So she devised a plan. She would come down to the pastry kitchen for a chat around five each evening and wait. Then as soon as the chefs received word that the family would be having a barbecue for dinner, Princess Diana would leave the kitchen and head for the nursery, promptly giving the nanny, Nanny Barnes, the night off. The princess could then have supper with the boys and get them into bed. The nursery had its own menu and she and the boys would have a grand time eating her childhood favorites like cottage pie and pudding. Of course, when Prince Charles came in to say "We are out for dinner tonight," it was too late. With the nanny unavailable, Princess Diana had the perfect excuse to stay in.

Meeting a Princess

Pastry Chef Robert Pine had the night off. I was told to suggest to the Duke, when he came into the kitchen, that there was apple pie and ice cream for dessert or alternatively, the Queen's freshly picked berries with ice cream. I memorized this little spiel and felt ready to speak to the Duke. No problem. So, it caught me by surprise when Princess Diana walked into the kitchen asking for a yogurt. All I could think of was, *Well she isn't the Duke, I'm supposed to speak to the Duke, for godsake! Where will she sit, where is she going to eat her yogurt, is there a spoon anywhere?*

Me with Robert Pine, the Queen's pastry chef at Balmoral. It was the first time I met Princess Diana.

Flustered, I turned around and banged my head into some flan rings that hung over the prep table. The princess burst out laughing. I managed to collect myself and get the princess her yogurt and she found a spot to sit on the chest freezer, all the while eating and chatting with me. Suddenly the Duke showed and exclaimed, "Aha! Caught you!" pointing a finger at Princess Diana. She laughed, slid off the freezer and walked out of the kitchen.

After that, the princess came by fairly frequently to get a snack or to chat. She would always sit on the chest freezer since there really wasn't anyplace else. In fact, we used the freezer top as a kind of shelf and would put cakes and tarts on it until we needed to serve them. If there was a fruit cake cooling on the freezer, Princess Diana would sit and chat with us, all the while picking out the raisins from the cake. It would be in crumbs by the time she left.

The Ghillies Ball

The Ghillies Ball was a twice-a-year event at Balmoral. The term *ghillie* is Gaelic for *gamekeeper*, and the ball was a Scottish dance party held as a thank you to the staff for all their hard work and every member of the royal family in residence and their guests would attend. The Queen's pipe major would announce the first dance, usually starting with a "Dashing White Sergeant"—a traditional dance where two women dance with one man.

Scottish dances are similar to square dances in that you are passed from partner to partner, ultimately getting to dance with everyone in the room. Prince Charles and Princess Diana especially enjoyed themselves. They both knew all the steps and Prince Charles would spin Princess Diana around faster and faster. They had a great time and it seemed to me that they were deeply in love.

During one Ghillies Ball, I was with my buddies in the corner when suddenly the group parted to make way for Princess Diana. "Darren, come dance with me," she said. I felt my face go beet red.

"But Your Royal Highness," I blurted out, "I don't know how."

"Oh, it's easy," she smiled. "I'll show you." She grabbed my arm and pulled me onto the floor as the pipe major announced a St. Bernard's waltz. Well, I had no idea who St. Bernard was, much less that he had a waltz named after him. The princess was a great dancer and she tried to show me the steps. She soon realized I was hopeless, so to tease me, she spun me around and started asking everyone to get out of the way. "Make way, coming through!" she hollered at Prince Andrew. She spun me toward the Queen. For a chilling moment I thought she was going to pass me off to Her Majesty but instead, she spun me past her. I had received my comeuppance.

Every year thereafter Princess Diana made a point to dance with me at the Ghillies Ball.

CURRIED SALMON KEDGEREE

Hearty breakfasts before a morning in the icy cold winds and rains of the highlands were a necessity. This kedgeree fits the bill. Salmon trimmings from the freshly caught fish are lightly poached and added to basmati rice, reduced cream, and spices, then topped with hard-boiled eggs and fresh parsley. It is better made with center cut salmon, with those big pink flakes poking out of the creamy rice. Often this dish would be requested for nursery breakfast, without the curry, but with lots of crispy bacon. We sometimes used smoked haddock, if it was available, instead of salmon.

1	quart water		Salt and freshly ground pepper
1	cup basmati rice	1½	pounds salmon, poached, then cooled and flaked
2	cups heavy cream or half-and-half		
1	tablespoon curry powder, or to taste	¼	cup finely chopped green onions
4	hard-boiled eggs, peeled	2	tablespoons finely chopped fresh parsley

1. Bring the water to a rolling boil in a 6-quart pot, and add the rice. Cook until the rice is tender, and then drain the rice in a colander. Return the pan to the heat, and add the cream and curry powder. Simmer until the cream starts to thicken slightly. Warm the eggs by placing them in a small pan of simmering water (about 3 cups). Shut off the heat, and let the eggs steep in the water for a few minutes.

2. Add the rice to the curried cream and stir. Once the rice is hot, season with the salt and pepper and stir in the flaked salmon gently, taking care not to break up the salmon pieces.

3. Spoon the kedgeree into a warm serving dish and sprinkle with the green onions and parsley. Remove the eggs from the water and cut into quarters. Garnish the edges of the kedgeree with the eggs.

MAKES 4 SERVINGS

SALMON FISHCAKES

2 pounds red skin potatoes, peeled	1/2 cup all-purpose flour plus flour for dusting
4 tablespoons finely chopped fresh parsley	2 cups white bread crumbs or panko (Japanese-style bread crumbs)
1 teaspoon lemon juice	2 eggs, beaten
3/4 teaspoon salt	3 cups peanut oil, for deep frying
1/8 teaspoon freshly ground black pepper	Fried parsley, for garnish (optional)
1 egg yolk	Fresh tomato sauce (optional)
1 1/2 pound salmon fillet, poached and chilled	

1. Cover the potatoes with cold water in a 6-quart pot, and bring the water to a boil. Cook for 18 minutes, or until tender, drain the potatoes, and return them to the pot. Mash the potatoes until smooth, and add the parsley, lemon juice, salt, pepper, and egg yolk. Flake the salmon, and fold into the potato mixture, mixing gently. Allow the mixture to cool for at least 1 hour, or overnight in the refrigerator.

2. Dust your work surface with a little flour, less than a tablespoon, and shape the fishcakes into even-size balls. Form into neat cakes by pressing down gently with a spatula. Each cake should be about 2 1/2 inches by 1 inch.

3. Put the flour, bread crumbs, and eggs in three separate bowls lined up in a row. First dredge the salmon cakes in the flour, shaking off the excess. Then dip them into the beaten egg, and then roll them in the bread crumbs. Place the fishcakes on a clean dish and refrigerate for at least 30 minutes or up to 24 hours.

4. Add the peanut oil to a deep saucepan, and heat until hot but not smoking. Deep-fry the salmon cakes, a few at a time without crowding the pan, until golden brown on both sides. Lift out of the pan, gently blot onto a paper towel, and serve immediately with fried parsley (directions on page 129) and fresh tomato sauce if desired.

MAKES 12 CAKES OR 6 SERVINGS

*A royal breakfast: (from left to right) Curried Salmon Kedegree,
Poached Eggs en Croûte, Salmon Fishcakes with tomato sauce*

POACHED EGGS EN CROÛTE

Breakfasts were usually served buffet style, so it was necessary to create a "basket" for poached eggs to sit in, so that they could be easily lifted and protected from hardening too quickly from the heat of the hot plate. Fried bread is a must for any English breakfast. A slice of bread is dropped into the bacon grease and reheated until golden and crispy. This dish is a meal in itself when you place chopped crispy bacon in the bottom of the bread before placing the egg on top and a spoonful of hollandaise over the egg.

1	loaf dense white bread, not sliced	1	teaspoon salt
4	cups vegetable oil, for frying	4	eggs
1	quart boiling water	1	tablespoon chopped chives
1	tablespoon white wine vinegar		

1. Trim the crusts off the loaf, and cut the bread into four, 2-inch-thick slices. Reserve any leftover bread and crusts for bread crumbs. Using cookie cutters, cut a 2½-inch circle out of each thick slice. Then with a 2-inch cutter, cut three-fourths of the way down into the 2½-inch bread circle, but be careful not to cut all the way through. (This will be the "cup" for the egg.) Heat the vegetable oil to 350 degrees and drop in the bread "croûtes." Fry until golden on all sides, and remove the croûtes to a plate and paper towel; keep warm.

2. In a large pan, bring the water to a rolling boil and add the vinegar and salt. Carefully crack the eggs into the boiling water, or if you would prefer, crack the eggs into a teacup one at a time and tip into the water. Swish the water so that the eggs do not stick to the bottom of the pan and boil the eggs for about 4 minutes. While the eggs are cooking, carefully remove the center disk of each croûte, leaving a "basket" in the center.

3. Using a slotted spoon lift the eggs out of the water, and place one in the center of each croûte. Sprinkle with the chives to serve.

MAKES 4 SERVINGS

GRAVAD LAX WITH SAUCE SUEDOISE

Gravad lax, or "buried salmon," gets its name from seventeenth-century sailors who used to cover the salmon in salt and bury it in the sand to preserve it. Today we still cover and cure the fish in salt, but it's only buried in the back of the refrigerator for five days. This was served often at the palace as a first course, sliced on a bed of lettuce and served with the sauce. But it also was served as a canapé for receptions.

Lax

- 3   pounds Atlantic salmon fillet, preferably mid-cut
- 4   tablespoons kosher salt
- 4   tablespoons sugar
- 2   teaspoons crushed white peppercorns
- 1   cup firmly packed chopped fresh dill, divided

Sauce

- 3   egg yolks
- 3   tablespoons sugar
- 1/4   cup plus 1 tablespoon sweet German mustard
- 2   cups corn oil or other neutral flavored oil
-    Salt and freshly ground pepper
- 1   tablespoon red wine vinegar (optional)
-    Lemon wedges for garnish

1. Cut the salmon in half across the middle and pat dry with paper towels. Remove the skin from both pieces and save. In a small bowl mix the salt, 4 tablespoons sugar, peppercorns, and ½ cup dill until combined. Toss the cure mix over the fish, and rub it on. Lay a piece of plastic wrap large enough to accommodate the salmon flat on a counter. Place a layer of salmon skin on top of the plastic, lay the fish pieces on top of that, and pack on all the remaining cure mix that didn't stick on and around the salmon. Place the remaining piece of salmon skin on the top, and wrap the whole fish tightly in the plastic wrap.

2. Place the salmon on a tray and put another tray on top to weigh the fish down. Refrigerate. Turn the fish over once each day, and leave it to cure for 5 days.

3. After 5 days, unwrap the salmon, and wipe the cure mixture off the pieces of salmon. Discard the cure mixture along with the skin.

4. **For the sauce,** in a large bowl whisk the egg yolks until creamy. Add the remaining 3 tablespoons sugar and the mustard, and drizzle the oil in slowly to make a mayonnaise. Whisk in the remaining dill, and adjust the seasoning with salt and pepper. For a sauce with a bit more bite, add the red wine vinegar.

5. Slice the salmon wafer-thin onto a serving dish, garnish with fresh dill and lemon wedges, and serve the sauce alongside.

MAKES 8 TO 10 SERVINGS

COTTAGE PIE

This is classic British nursery food. Princes William and Harry demanded it at least once a week. Freshly ground beef in a rich brown sauce is topped with lightly whipped mashed potatoes flavored with nutmeg and melted cheese.

Beef base

2	tablespoons corn oil
2	small yellow onions, finely chopped
1¹/₂	pounds ground beef
¹/₃	cup all-purpose flour
1	to 2 teaspoons dried thyme
2¹/₂	cups water
1	tablespoon Kitchen Bouquet browning and seasoning sauce
2	beef bouillon cubes
1	tablespoon Worcestershire sauce

Potato topping

2¹/₂	pounds red potatoes (about 8 medium)
¹/₂	stick (¹/₄ cup) unsalted butter
2	teaspoons salt
¹/₈	teaspoon freshly ground black pepper
¹/₈	teaspoon grated nutmeg
¹/₄	cup heavy cream
1	egg yolk
1	cup grated cheddar cheese

1. Preheat the oven to 350 degrees.

2. For the beef base, heat the oil in a large saucepan over a high flame until warm, and add the finely chopped onion. Sauté until the onion becomes soft and translucent. Add the ground beef, breaking it up with a wooden spoon, and sauté until the beef has lost all its pink color. Gradually stir in the flour, thyme, water, Kitchen Bouquet, bouillon cubes, and Worcestershire sauce.

3. Reduce the heat to low and simmer the meat for 30 to 45 minutes, or until the sauce has thickened and the meat is tender. Remove the pan from the stove and using a slotted spoon, transfer the beef to a 3-quart ovenproof casserole dish. If there is any sauce left after taking out the meat, cool and refrigerate it. This juice can be reheated and served alongside the finished pie, if you like. The beef base can be prepared up to this point several days in advance and refrigerated.

4. For the potato topping, place the potatoes in a large pot, and add cold water an inch above the potatoes. Cover the pot and bring the potatoes to a boil over high heat. Lower the heat to a simmer, and cook until the potatoes are tender when pricked with a fork, about 20 minutes. Drain off the water and return the drained potatoes to

Cottage Pie (front), Queen of Puddings

the pan over low heat for 1 to 2 minutes to dry them thoroughly. Mash the potatoes with a potato masher, or pass them through a ricer.

5. Stir the nutmeg, cream, egg yolk, butter, salt, and pepper into the mashed potatoes. Either pipe the mashed potatoes on top of the beef using a wide star tube, or spoon the potatoes on top and fluff them up using a fork.

6. Sprinkle the grated cheddar over the potatoes, and bake for 20 to 30 minutes, or until the potatoes are golden brown and the pie has heated through. If you don't want to cook the cottage pie right away, it can be made a day ahead, covered with plastic wrap, and refrigerated.

MAKES 4 SERVINGS

MARINATED PORTABELLA MUSHROOMS

In the UK we call portabellas "flat" mushrooms. A standard vegetable order from the royal kitchens would include so many boxes of "flats" and so many of "buttons." This was, of course, before Antonio Carluccio introduced us to "wild mushrooms."

4	large portabella mushrooms		1	teaspoon finely chopped green onions
1/2	cup olive oil		1/4	teaspoon dried thyme
1	tablespoon Worcestershire sauce		1	clove garlic, crushed
2	tablespoons tarragon vinegar		1/4	teaspoon salt
2	tablespoons red wine (optional)		1/4	teaspoon freshly ground black pepper

1. Preheat the oven to 350 degrees. Peel the skin off the mushrooms to allow the marinade to seep into the flesh. Carefully remove the center stem out of the mushrooms. (This piece is too dense and the gills would be long cooked before this piece would be tender.) Then cut the mushrooms into halves on the bias for presentation purposes. Whisk together the olive oil, Worcestershire sauce, vinegar, red wine, green onions, thyme, garlic, salt, and pepper, and pour into a ziplock bag. Add the mushrooms, and marinate at room temperature for about 1 hour, turning the bag occasionally.

2. Place the mushrooms onto a baking sheet and cook in the center of the oven until tender, 15 to 20 minutes. Serve warm or at room temperature.

MAKES 4 SERVINGS

STEAK DIANE

This classic 1970s dish is still popular with the royal family and is one the Duke of Edinburgh loved to cook for family barbecues. We would prepare the ingredients, flatten the steaks in advance, and send it all to the barbecue site in yellow Tupperware boxes. The contents of each Tupperware container were labeled, at least in theory. Occasionally a label was missing and believe me, we heard all about it from the Duke the next day.

4	(4-ounce) beef tenderloin steaks	1/2	cube beef bouillon
	Salt and freshly ground pepper	1	teaspoon Worcestershire sauce
4	tablespoons olive oil, divided	2	tablespoons brandy
1	cup finely chopped onion	1	tablespoon finely chopped fresh
1	cup sliced button mushrooms		chives
1	cup heavy cream		

1. Flatten each steak with a rolling pin to about ½ inch thick. Season with salt and pepper to taste. Add 2 tablespoons olive oil to a sauté pan large enough to accommodate the steaks in one layer. Heat the oil until hot, but not smoking. Cook the steaks on high heat for about 2 minutes on each side. Remove from the skillet onto a plate and keep warm.

2. Add the remaining 2 tablespoons olive oil to the pan, and add the onion, sautéing until it softens. Stir in the mushrooms and sauté until soft. Stir in the cream, beef bouillon, Worcestershire sauce, and brandy. Increase the heat to reduce the liquid to the consistency of heavy cream. Remove the sauce from the heat, and check the seasoning for taste. Return the steaks to the pan along with the juices, and cover with the sauce for 1 or 2 minutes just to reheat the steaks. Serve sprinkled with the chopped chives for garnish.

MAKES 4 SERVINGS

TENDERLOIN STEAKS STUFFED WITH BOURSIN WITH A ROSEMARY, BELL PEPPER SAUCE

Sauce

2	tablespoons butter
2	tablespoons olive oil
1/2	medium red bell pepper, cut into 1-inch strips
1/2	medium red bell pepper, chopped
1	small onion, finely chopped
2	sprigs fresh rosemary
2	cloves garlic, crushed
3	tablespoons all-purpose flour
1	beef bouillon cube
1/2	teaspoon Kitchen Bouquet browning and seasoning sauce
2	cups water
1	teaspoon tomato paste
	Salt and freshly ground pepper

Steaks

4	tenderloin steaks, about 6 ounces each
4	ounces Boursin cheese
2	tablespoons pine nuts, toasted
	Salt and pepper
1	tablespoon olive oil
2	tablespoons chopped green onions

1. Preheat the oven to 400 degrees.

2. **For the sauce**, melt the butter and oil in a large sauté pan over medium heat. Add the pepper strips and sauté until tender. Remove the bell pepper and set aside for garnish. Add the chopped peppers, onions, garlic, rosemary, and a pinch of salt to the sauté pan and cook until they start to soften and brown. Stir in the flour and continue to sauté for a minute. Add the bouillon cube, browning sauce, tomato paste, and water, and keep stirring until the sauce forms. Simmer for at least 20 minutes. Strain the sauce, discarding the cooked vegetables, and add the salt and pepper to taste. Keep the sauce warm until the steaks are cooked. Alternatively, allow the sauce to cool and refrigerate it for up to 24 hours.

3. **For the steaks**, make a 2-inch slit in the side of each steak, and stuff the pocket with an equal mixture of Boursin and pine nuts. Season the steaks with salt and freshly ground pepper to taste, and allow them to come to room temperature. Add the olive oil to a large sauté pan until hot, but not smoking. Add the steaks, and cook for about 2 minutes on each side. Remove and place the pan in the oven for 10 minutes or until done to your liking.

4. Remove the steaks from the oven and let them rest for 5 minutes. Place some warm sauce on a clean plate, top with the steak, and garnish with the reserved red pepper strips and freshly chopped green onions.

MAKES 4 SERVINGS

Grilling with the Duke—Tenderloin Steaks Stuffed with Boursin with a Rosemary, Bell Pepper Sauce, Marinated Portabella Mushrooms, Greek Yogurt and Strawberry Cheesecake

POACHED SALMON WITH DILL HOLLANDAISE

Dill Hollandaise

1½ sticks (¾ cup) unsalted butter
3   egg yolks
1   teaspoon water
1   lemon, juiced
2   teaspoons chopped fresh dill
    Salt and freshly ground black pepper

Salmon

2   quarts (8 cups) cold water
12   black peppercorns, crushed
4   carrots, peeled and thinly sliced
3   small onions, peeled and thinly sliced
2   ribs celery, washed and thinly sliced
1   tablespoon salt
1   tablespoon white wine vinegar
4   stems fresh parsley
1   bay leaf
1   sprig fresh thyme or 1 pinch of dried thyme
1½   pounds Atlantic salmon fillet, skinned and cut into 4 pieces

1. **For the dill hollandaise**, melt the butter in a small pan over low heat. It will separate into three parts. On the bottom will be the milk solids, in the middle the clear clarified butter, and on the top the foamy milk solids. Carefully skim off the top foamy solids and discard.

2. Set a metal bowl over a pan of simmering water. The bowl should not touch the water. Whisk the eggs and water together for 30 seconds, or until warm and slightly frothy. Remove the bowl and slowly whisk in the clarified butter, but not the milk solids at the bottom, to form a thick emulsion. After the butter has been beaten into the eggs, gradually add the lemon juice. Then add the dill and the salt and pepper to taste. Keep the sauce warm until ready to use.

3. **For the salmon**, place the peppercorns, carrots, onions, and celery along with the salt, vinegar, parsley, bay leaf, and thyme into a 10-quart pot, and simmer for 20 minutes, or until aromatic. Strain the liquid and discard the cooked vegetables. Bring the liquid (now called a court bouillon) to a boil in large sauté pan. The liquid should be several inches deep. Add the salmon and then reduce the heat so that the bouillon barely simmers. Cover the pan, and gently poach the salmon for about 6 minutes. Remove the salmon with a slotted spoon, and allow it to cool on a wire rack or serving dish.

4. Salmon can be served at room temperature or chilled. Accompany with the Dill Hollandaise.

MAKES 4 SERVINGS

GOUJONS OF SALMON WITH TYROLIENNE SAUCE

Goujons of salmon and crème brûlée were the two most requested dishes by Prince Andrew. The goujons were really popular in the nursery too—though we had to send up ketchup instead of the Sauce Tyrolienne. Because the fish can be breaded up to a day ahead, it was often made for receptions and was one of our "best sellers." Don't feel bound to use salmon. The royal family enjoyed a mixture of fried fish like salmon, smoked haddock, and Dover sole. Then it was listed on the menu as "panachee de fruits de mer," but you can also call it a more common name—"fried fish fingers with tartar sauce"!

4 cups vegetable oil, for frying	1/4 cup tomato ketchup
1 1/2 pounds center-cut salmon, skinned	1 tablespoon finely chopped fresh parsley
1 cup all-purpose flour	1 tablespoon finely chopped capers
2 eggs, beaten	1 tablespoon finely chopped cornichons
3 cups panko or dried white bread crumbs	Salt and freshly ground pepper
3/4 cup mayonnaise	1 small bunch parsley

1. Preheat the oil in a heavy-bottomed pan or deep fryer to 375 degrees. Cut the salmon into finger-size pieces, about 2 1/2 x 1/2 inches. Place the flour, panko, and egg onto three separate dinner plates. Dredge the salmon fingers first through the flour, then the egg, and finally the panko. Do this a few at a time so that they don't stick together. Lay them on a baking sheet until all are coated. Discard any remaining flour, egg, or panko.

2. **For the sauce,** in a large bowl mix the mayonnaise, ketchup, parsley, capers, and cornichons. Season with the salt and pepper to taste.

3. Carefully drop the salmon fingers into the hot oil, taking care not to crowd the pan, and fry them until golden and crisp, about 3 to 4 minutes. Lift out with a slotted spoon onto a paper towel to drain. Keep warm while you cook the remaining fingers.

4. Break the parsley bunch into tiny sprigs, and drop all together into the hot oil. After 30 seconds, lift out with a slotted spoon onto a paper towel to drain. Serve the goujons sprinkled with the fried parsley and accompanied by the dipping sauce.

MAKES 4 SERVINGS

GLENFIDDICH CHOCOLATE MOUSSE

Put anything chocolate on the menu and Her Majesty would usually give it an affirmative check in the Menu Book. This dense mousse was one of her favorites. Although the Queen is not a big whiskey drinker, Glenfiddich—"valley of the deer" in Gaelic—whiskey from the Scottish highlands adds a warm aftertaste. The coffee intensifies the flavor. You can substitute crème de menthe for the whiskey. If you don't want to use alcohol, then fold finely chopped crystallized ginger or even a few chocolate chips through the mix.

6	ounces semisweet chocolate
1	teaspoon instant coffee
1	tablespoon boiling water
5	eggs, separated
2	tablespoons Glenfiddich whiskey

1¼	cups heavy cream
1	cup heavy cream, whipped for garnish
2	ounces grated semisweet chocolate, for garnish

1. Melt the 6 ounces of chocolate in a double boiler or, alternatively, microwave it on high for 1 minute and stir until melted. In a small bowl dissolve the coffee into the boiling water.

2. Whisk the egg yolks into the melted chocolate and then stir in the dissolved coffee and the whiskey and mix well.

3. Whip the cream until it forms and holds stiff peaks. Whip the egg whites until they form and hold stiff peaks. Fold the whipped cream and whipped egg whites into the chocolate mixture. Keep folding until you can no longer see any white specks of cream or egg white.

4. Pour the mousse into a decorative serving dish, and refrigerate for at least 3 hours to allow the chocolate to set. Decorate the top of the mousse with rosettes of whipped cream and grated chocolate.

MAKES 6 SERVINGS

SCOTTISH THISTLE SHORTBREAD

This recipe has literally been used for centuries. At Balmoral we made it every day, and it was a perfect tea cake. It was a favorite of the Queen's niece, Lady Sarah, who would tuck six whole shortbreads into her luggage at the end of each visit. Dusted with vanilla sugar, it crumbles into eight portions and can be served as a tea cake, alone or with homemade ice cream. If you don't have traditional beechwood shortbread molds you can bake this in ceramic molds or roll the dough into a log and cut 1/2-inch cookies.

1 1/2 cups all-purpose flour

3/4 cup cornstarch

1 cup powdered sugar

2 sticks unsalted butter

1/4 cup vanilla sugar (see page 76)

1. Preheat the oven to 350 degrees. Place a sheet of parchment paper on a baking sheet. Sift the flour, cornstarch, and powdered sugar into a large bowl. Cut the butter into small pieces and rub them into the flour mixture until it forms into a ball. Lightly dust a shortbread mold with flour and press the dough into the mold. Trim off any excess. If using a beechwood mold, mold the shortbread and then tip it out onto the parchment paper, and prick the top of the shortbread all over with a fork before baking. If using a ceramic mold, bake the shortbread directly in the mold.

2. Bake in the preheated oven for 20 minutes, or until golden brown. Remove from the oven and mark the shortbread into wedges with a knife, cutting about one-third of the way through. Sprinkle with the vanilla sugar, and place on a cooling rack to cool completely.

MAKES 8 TO 10 SERVINGS

SUMMER PUDDING

By August, the Balmoral gardens are bursting with late season fruit and berries, especially strawberries. All this bounty meant that Summer Pudding would be on the menu at least once a week. The royal family loved to take this out on picnics and would spoon it right out of the dish.

2	pounds mixed berries—cherries, strawberries, raspberries, red currants, black currants, blackberries, blueberries	1½	cups sugar
½	cup water	8	slices dense white bread, several days old
1	teaspoon vanilla paste		Sprigs of fresh mint, for garnish
			Clotted cream

1. Prepare the fruit by stoning and halving the cherries, removing stems from the red and black currants, and hulling and quartering the strawberries. Keep each type of fruit separate at this stage.

2. In a large heavy-bottomed pan add the cherries, water, vanilla paste, and sugar over a low heat, and stir until the sugar dissolves. Let the cherries simmer until they start to soften. Add the strawberries and blackberries and stir; simmer 2 to 3 minutes, and then add the blueberries, red currants, black currants, and finally the raspberries. Remove from the heat, and carefully strain the fruit into a colander, reserving the poaching syrup in a separate bowl.

3. Cut the crusts off the bread, and cut a circle from 1 slice of the bread to fit the bottom of the pudding basin. Dip the bread into the poaching syrup and place it into a 1-quart pudding basin or soufflé dish. Cut all but 2 of the remaining 7 bread slices in half, dip them into the syrup, and line the sides of the basin, overlapping each piece slightly.

4. Once the basin is completely lined, spoon the fruit into the center and fill the basin to the top. Place the 2 remaining pieces of bread on top of the fruit. Place a saucer that fits snugly inside the basin on top of the bread. Weigh down the top of the pudding by placing something like a large can of tomatoes on top of the saucer. Refrigerate 6 to 8 hours or overnight along with any remaining poaching syrup.

5. Run a spatula around the edges of the pudding, and invert it onto a serving plate. Pour the remaining syrup over the top, and allow the syrup to run down the sides. Garnish with sprigs of mint and serve with the clotted cream.

Summer Pudding

MAKES 6 SERVINGS

CRATHIE CRUNCH

Named after the village next to Balmoral Castle, this cheesecake was popular to send out on shooting lunches. It is a crunchy layer of chocolate cookies and unsalted butter topped with a cheesecake batter flavored with crème de menthe. As a baroque final touch, we would top it with whipped cream and crumbled chocolate mint candy. Nestle's peppermint chocolate Aero Bar is my first choice since it has the right lightness and crunch. If you can't find that, a good dusting of grated chocolate is a more-than-acceptable substitute.

1/2   pound (8 ounces) McVities chocolate digestives or 1 cup ground graham cracker crumbs mixed with 1/2 cup grated bittersweet chocolate

6   tablespoons unsalted butter, melted

4   eggs, separated

2   tablespoons crème de menthe liqueur

2/3   cup granulated sugar

2   packets unflavored gelatin

1   tablespoon water

1 1/2   cups heavy cream

1   peppermint chocolate Aero Bar or 1/3 cup grated chocolate

1. Grind the cookies in a food processor until fine crumbs form. Place in a large bowl and stir in the melted butter. Firmly pack the mixture into the bottom of a 9-inch tart pan and refrigerate for at least 15 minutes.

2. Place the egg yolks, crème de menthe, and sugar into a large mixing bowl over a pan of boiling water, and whisk for about 2 minutes. Remove the bowl from the heat, and continue whisking until the mixture is cold.

3. Soften the gelatin in the 1 tablespoon water in a small pan, and place over low heat to warm and dissolve the gelatin. Whisk the gelatin into the egg mixture.

4. Whip the egg whites until stiff, and fold into the egg mixture. Spoon this onto the tart crust, and refrigerate for at least 2 hours.

5. Whip the heavy cream in a large bowl until stiff, and spread onto the top of the now-set egg mix. Chop the mint chocolate bar, and decorate with it or the grated chocolate.

MAKES 8 SERVINGS

Crathie Crunch

BREAD AND BUTTER PUDDING

This pudding was Princess Diana's all-time favorite, so much so that she once had a royal reporter write that "Darren makes the best bread and butter pudding in the world." Well, I am not sure it is the best in the world—but it's up there! The final texture is a cross between a bread pudding and a crème brûlée.

3	ounces raisins	3/4	cup sugar
1/4	cup Amaretto	1/2	cup milk
12	slices white bread, crusts removed	2	cups heavy cream
1 1/2	sticks unsalted butter, melted	2	tablespoons granulated sugar, to dust top of pudding
9	egg yolks	3	ounces sliced almonds, lightly toasted
2	teaspoons vanilla paste	2	tablespoons powdered sugar

1. Soak the raisins in the Amaretto, and leave covered with plastic wrap at room temperature 6 to 8 hours or overnight.

2. Preheat the oven to 350 degrees. Cut 4 slices of the bread into 1/2-inch dice, and spread the diced bread on the bottom of a casserole dish. Sprinkle the raisins on top of the bread cubes, and pour any remaining liquid over the bread. Cut the remaining 8 slices of bread in half diagonally, and then cut each half slice in half diagonally to create 4 even triangles per slice. Dip the triangles into the butter, and arrange on the top of the raisins, overlapping the triangles slightly. Pour any remaining butter over the top of the bread.

3. Whisk the yolks, vanilla paste, and sugar in a large bowl until combined. Bring the milk and cream to a boil in a heavy saucepan over high heat, and pour the hot mix onto the egg yolks, whisking constantly. Pour the warm egg mixture over the bread, making sure all of the bread is coated, and set aside the coated bread for 20 minutes to allow the egg mixture to soak into the bread.

4. Place the casserole dish in a roasting tray filled with hot water halfway up the sides of the casserole dish, and bake on the middle rack in the oven for 30 to 45 minutes, or until golden brown on top with the filling just set.

5. Remove the dish from the oven and roasting tray, and sprinkle with the extra sugar. Broil or use a crème brûlée torch to caramelize the sugar. Sprinkle with the toasted sliced almonds, and dust with powdered sugar. Cool slightly, and serve warm with a jug of cream and some fresh berries.

Bread and Butter Pudding

MAKES 6 TO 8 SERVINGS.

GREEK YOGURT AND STRAWBERRY CHEESECAKE

This cheesecake works well with other fruit besides strawberries. I would sometimes use blueberries as a topping. Arrange them neatly in circles covering the top of the cheesecake and drizzle with honey before serving.

Crust

6	tablespoons unsalted butter, melted
1½	cups graham cracker crumbs
1	cup finely chopped pecans
¼	cup light brown sugar
1	lemon, zest only

Cheesecake

1	cup cottage cheese
1	(7-ounce) container thick Greek yogurt
½	cup sugar
1	teaspoon vanilla paste
2	cups heavy cream, whipped until stiff
1	packet unflavored gelatin
3	tablespoons lemon juice, about 1 lemon
4	cups strawberries, sliced
½	cup vanilla sugar (see page 76)

1. **For the crust,** line a 13 x 9-inch baking sheet with parchment paper. Prepare the crust by mixing the butter, graham crumbs, pecans, brown sugar, and lemon zest together in a large bowl. Spread evenly onto the lined baking sheet and press down firmly. Refrigerate for at least 1 hour.

2. **For the cheesecake,** blend the cheese in a processor until smooth. Add the yogurt, sugar, and vanilla, and blend again. Transfer the mix to a large bowl, and fold in the whipped cream.

3. Dissolve the gelatin with the lemon juice in a small pan, and heat until the gelatin softens. Pour the gelatin into the cheese mix, and stir in quickly to avoid any lumps. Spread the cheesecake mix over the crumb base and refrigerate for about 2 hours.

4. Mix the strawberries with the vanilla sugar and leave to infuse for about 30 minutes. Arrange neatly on top of the cheesecake.

MAKES 8 SERVINGS

PEACH PRINCESS

This dish was a great way of using up the Windsor peaches that were too bruised for the dessert dishes. We also made it using pears instead of peaches. At Balmoral we had to double the recipe and pour one half into a silver jet and the other half into a yellow plastic Tupperware container—just in case there was a BBQ and they wanted to take the dish with them. Note that you'll make double the amount of Jell-O you need. That's all right, the kids will love the treat!

1 packet unflavored gelatin	1 (3-ounce box) lemon Jell-O
1¼ cups whole milk, divided	2 cups water, divided
2 eggs, separated	3/4 cup heavy cream
1/3 cup sugar	3 ripe peaches, skinned and halved
1 teaspoon vanilla paste	Extra whipped cream

1. In a large bowl dissolve the gelatin in ¼ cup milk. Whisk the egg yolks, sugar, and vanilla paste in a large bowl until combined. Bring the remaining 1 cup milk to a boil in a heavy-bottomed saucepan. Remove from the heat, and slowly pour the milk into the egg yolk mixture, whisking constantly. Pour the mixture back into the saucepan, stirring over low heat until it starts to thicken and coat the back of the spoon. Remove from the heat, pour the egg mixture over the dissolved gelatin, and whisk until combined. Strain the gelatin mix through a fine strainer into a large bowl, and refrigerate until cold and just starting to set, about 1 hour. This will become a custard. Be careful not to let the mix chill for too long, or it will set firm.

2. Empty the box of lemon Jell-O into a bowl. Bring 1 cup water to a boil, and pour it over the lemon Jell-O, stirring to dissolve. Add 1 cup cold water, and refrigerate until the Jell-O starts to set, about 1 hour.

3. Whip the cream until stiff peaks form. In a separate bowl, whip the egg whites until stiff, and carefully fold them into the custard mix along with the whipped cream. Spoon into a soufflé dish, and refrigerate the mousse until firm.

4. Cut each peach in half and remove the pits. Lay each half cut-side down on top of the mousse uniformly. Spoon half of the lemon Jell-O mix over the peaches and mousse so that the layer is about ¼ inch deep. Refrigerate until set. Garnish with whipped cream.

MAKES 6 SERVINGS

OLD ENGLISH APPLE PIE

1. Preheat the oven to 350 degrees.

Pastry

2½	sticks (1¼ cups) unsalted butter
3/4	cup sugar
1	egg
1	teaspoon vanilla paste
3	cups all-purpose flour

Filling

4	Granny Smith apples
1/2	cup granulated sugar
1/4	cup Muscovado sugar
1/3	cup raisins
1/2	stick unsalted butter, melted and cooled
1	lemon, juice and zest
1	orange, juice and zest
1/2	teaspoon ground nutmeg
1	teaspoon ground cinnamon
1	egg, beaten

2. **For the pastry,** cream the butter and sugar until smooth, and add the egg and vanilla paste. Add the flour and blend until combined. Refrigerate for at least one hour.

3. **For the filling,** peel, core, and slice the apples. Place the apples in a large bowl, and add the granulated sugar, Muscovado sugar, raisins, melted butter, lemon and orange zests and juice, nutmeg, and cinnamon. Stir until combined.

4. Divide the dough in half. Roll out the bottom crust, and fit it into a 9-inch pie pan or a 9 x 1½-inch flan ring. Place the apple filling inside. Brush the edge of the pastry with the beaten egg. Roll out the top crust, place it on the bottom crust and trim the edges. Brush the remaining egg over the top of the pie. Bake in the center of the oven for 40 minutes, or until the pastry is golden brown.

MAKES 6 SERVINGS

VEILED FARMER'S DAUGHTER

This strangely named dish was published in a national newspaper and sounded good. I was always on the lookout for new recipes that contained strawberries because the royal family ate them so often when in season. I tweaked the recipe and listed it in the Menu Book, forgetting to put the recipe in alongside for Her Majesty to peruse. I shouldn't have been surprised when I received the note below in the Menu Book when it returned to the kitchen.

6	slices whole wheat bread, crusts removed	2	pounds ripe strawberries, raspberries, or a combination of both
2	teaspoons ground cinnamon	1	orange, zest and juice
6	tablespoons Demerara sugar	2	tablespoons Curaçao
2	cups heavy cream		
4	tablespoons vanilla sugar (see page 76), divided		

1. Preheat the oven to 350 degrees. Pulse the bread in a food processor until fine crumbs form, and mix with the cinnamon and Demerara sugar. Spread onto a baking sheet and bake for about 10 minutes, or until the bread becomes crisp and golden. Remove from the oven, and stir the crumbs, leaving them on the baking sheet until cool.

2. Whip the heavy cream with 2 tablespoons vanilla sugar. Hull and halve the strawberries into a bowl, and toss with the remaining 2 tablespoons vanilla sugar and the orange zest and juice. Drizzle with the Curaçao.

3. In a large glass serving bowl, place a layer of the fruit followed by a layer of the whipped cream and sprinkle on some of the sugared crumbs. Repeat the process and build the layers, finishing with the cream and a heavy sprinkling of the crumbs.

MAKES 6 SERVINGS

What or who are the Veiled Farmers Daughter?!

QUEEN OF PUDDINGS

This pudding originated at Buckingham Palace in the seventeenth century and was created for Queen Victoria by the palace chefs. The version below is updated from the original and is one I used at Buckingham Palace and Kensington Palace for Princes William and Harry. Princess Diana, not a huge dessert eater, would occasionally succumb to a taste as well.

1 small Sara Lee pound cake, cut into 1/2-inch slices	2 cups whole milk
4 eggs	1 (12-ounce) jar strawberry jelly
1 1/2 cups granulated sugar, divided	4 egg whites, at room temperature
1 teaspoon vanilla paste	1/4 cup sliced almonds

1. Preheat the oven to 350 degrees. Cover the bottom of an 8-inch casserole dish with the pound cake slices. In a large bowl, beat together the whole eggs, 1/2 cup sugar, and the vanilla paste until light and lemon colored. Bring the milk to a boil in a small saucepan, remove it from the heat, and slowly whisk the hot milk into the eggs and sugar mixture. Gently pour the mixture into the casserole dish, making sure you soak all of the pound cake as it rises to the top. Put the casserole dish in the oven and bake for 30 minutes, or until it is firmly set. Remove the dish from the oven and allow it to cool slightly.

2. In a small saucepan, warm the strawberry jelly and pour it over the top of the warm pudding.

3. Make a meringue by whisking the egg whites until stiff, adding the remaining 1 cup sugar gradually. The standing mixer with a balloon whisk attachment does a great job here. After the sugar has been fully incorporated into the whites, and the whites are stiff and glossy, spoon the meringue mixture into a piping bag with a star tip and pipe around the edges of the casserole on top of the jelly. Then make a trellis across the middle of the dish to leave some of the red jelly showing between the meringue. Sprinkle the almonds on top of the meringue.

4. Return the casserole dish to the oven for about 10 minutes until the meringue and almonds start to brown. Serve hot with whipped cream or ice cream.

MAKES 6 SERVINGS

BALMORAL STRAWBERRY JAM

Balmoral was the only place we made jams and jellies, and we would have enough fruit from the Balmoral gardens to make enough to last a year. Jam was usually made on a Sunday morning. It was the one day each week we could be certain that lunch would be in the house, not outdoors. No one ever shot or hunted on the Sabbath. Nothing worse than having to put together a plum pudding for a shooting lunch just as your jam hits 220 degrees.

This homemade jam technique is different from most, since there is no final hot water bath to seal the jar. The heat from the hot jam seals the jar and no further processing is required.

4 cups strawberries, hulled (not overripe and not washed)	3 tablespoons lemon juice
1 3/4 cups granulated sugar	1 tablespoon vanilla paste

1. Sterilize a 12-ounce jelly jar, screw-on top, and lid in boiling water. Remove from the water and turn the lid upside down, allowing it to dry. Keep the jar warm so that it doesn't crack when you pour in the hot jam.

2. Cut the strawberries in half and add them to an 8-quart saucepan with the sugar, lemon juice, and vanilla paste. Place the pan over a high heat, and stir the strawberries until the sugar starts to dissolve. Bring the jam mixture to a rolling boil until the temperature reaches 220°F on a candy thermometer.

3. Remove the pan from the heat, stir, and let cool for 10 minutes. Pour the jam into the warm jar, place the lid on top, and tighten the screw band. Turn the jar upside down for about 30 minutes and then right side up until it cools completely. This will stop all of the berries from sinking to the bottom of the jar. Once the jar is cold, test the lid by pressing the top. If it springs back, it needs to be refrigerated and used within a week. If the lid doesn't spring back, then the jam will keep for up to one year.

Remember, don't put your labels on until the jam is cooled. Otherwise the glue backing will melt right off.

MAKES ONE 12-OUNCE JAR

CHAPTER SIX

Sandringham House

A Royal Christmas

Sandringham House, where the Windsors celebrate Christmas and New Year, is one of the most beautiful homes in England. The house is a mix of styles, mostly Victorian, and sits on sixty acres of stunning gardens with considerable acreage set aside for a wonderful apple orchard. On the property there is a converted stable that houses a museum of royal vehicles and memorabilia and two smaller homes, Wood Farm and Park House.

Inside the house are royal collections of porcelain, jade, furniture, and priceless family portraits. In many ways, Sandringham epitomizes English country living and is a perfect place for the Windsor family to be together for the holidays.

Sandringham House was my favorite royal residence. The house is elegant and the grounds, situated on flat Norfolk land, provide beautiful views wherever you cast your gaze. The kitchen was like the rest of the house—warm, welcoming, easy to spend time in.

The Queen had always used Sandringham for her New Year's celebrations. But after the fire at Windsor, her stay at Sandringham was extended to include Christmas. So now the Windsors stay at Sandringham from December 23 through the end of January. At Christmas the house is decorated with holly leaves and berries and a twenty-foot Norfolk pine has been chopped down on the estate and sits inside the White Drawing Room, glittering with decorations. The fireplaces are blazing with log fires and even though it may be cold and snowy outside, everyone feels warm and pampered inside.

The chefs and other staff arrive at Sandringham around December 20 to ready the house. As chefs we know that we'll be feeding one hundred forty people four meals a day, so we immediately prep our meat and fish, check on the vegetable orders, and make several dozen mince pies to freeze and bake later. Besides pies, I'd also make several ganache-covered Yule logs for the nursery and the royal dining room. One year I decorated the nursery Yule log with a fat marzipan Father Christmas squashing Rudolph. There was a more sedate log with a spray of marzipan poinsettias for the grown-ups.

Most of the royal family doesn't arrive until Christmas Eve. Their Range Rovers drive to the large front entrance, depositing the family into the house's main sitting room called the Saloon. Then the chauffeurs swing to the side of the house and the real unloading begins. It's backstairs bedlam. Personal valets, assisted by the Queen's traveling yeoman, are directing luggage up to the rooms. Christmas gifts are transferred from each car to the white linen-covered trestle tables in the White Drawing Room, which have name cards and ribbons indicating where each person's presents should be placed. There are hampers of food making their way into the kitchen, either brought personally by the royals, or received as gifts and shared.

I remember each year the Sultan of Brunei would send over an enormous Fortnum & Mason hamper, filled with sugared dried fruits, hams, cheeses, and biscuits for the Queen, and perhaps also for Prince Charles and Prince Andrew. Besides that, friends know that the Windsors are always happy to receive gifts of food and drink, so there are plenty of special liqueurs, pâtés, smoked turkeys, and rare cheeses that make their way to the kitchen. Harrods always sent over an enormous hamper that faithfully contained a pâté de foie gras en Croûte. There are sweets and lots of candy. One teatime treat that the whole family adores are cookies called "Chocolate Olivers." They are round, dark-chocolate-dipped cookies that come in a long telescope-like box.

Not Your Typical Fruitcake

Among the food we transported to Sandringham each Christmas were six royal Christmas cakes. The royal family would have one for Christmas and one for New Year's, ditto the nursery and the staff. "Christmas cake" is a euphemism for that often maligned gift called "fruitcake." Now before you groan and turn the page, I have to tell you that these are very, very good cakes.

They are started in October, just after the Balmoral summer holidays. Butter and sugar are creamed together before adding flour, eggs, molasses, ground almonds, and marinated dried fruit that have been soaked in brandy from the night before. The fruit is a combination of orange and lemon zests and juices, raisins, currants, sultanas, glacéed cherries, and citron peel.

The cakes are baked slowly for eight hours in a low oven, then pricked all over and soaked with brandy and sugar syrup. Wrapped in parchment and plastic, the cakes are stored in a cool place and "fed" more brandy and sugar syrup every few weeks. Their final decoration is fondant icing with additional flounces and frills. The flavor of the fruit, having been baptized in brandy, is rich and mellow. Now I promise that a gift of that cake with a tin of good tea will be greeted with gratitude, not groans.

Cakes decorated with Santa and his sleigh for the nursery and Santa climbing out of the chimney for the royal table. All in marzipan, of course. One cake has Sonic the Hedgehog on it, made the same year William and Harry got a PlayStation for Christmas. A Christmas cake shows Sandringham house in the snow, decorated by Robert Pine, the pastry chef.

Sneak Attack

William and Harry would get all sorts of athletic equipment, games, Nintendos and electronic toys, books, and crafts for Christmas. But I'll not forget the year they each received very large water guns. Well, those guns were a big hit. And the targets were usually the chefs! All Christmas week, we withstood sudden attacks from the boys. I would be preparing lunch in the kitchen and suddenly I was soaked with water. And they kept doing it. "That's it!" I would yell at the boys. "You are going to get it now!" But the boys would laugh and run away, carefully plotting out their next attack.

My chef mate, Arthur Smith, and I decided to fight back. We headed into town and found a fantastic local toy shop that sold water guns, black plastic replicas of Israeli Uzis. *These will be great,* we thought. *Finally a bit of comeuppance for those two.* We returned to Sandringham just as twilight was deepening and a thick snow had begun to fall. After a quick change into our chef whites we headed across the parking lot toward the kitchen with our water guns by our sides.

Three feet across the yard, I heard a click and a deep voice yell, "Freeze! Armed police!" We both froze. Out of nowhere an officer appeared. As he got closer he recognized us. Fortunately for us he was London police, not local.

"What have you got there?" he asked.

Before I could say anything, Arthur piped up, "Oh these? These are for William and Harry. We are going to shoot them as they come out of tea."

My mouth dropped open. That didn't sound right! I quickly explained that they were just water guns. The officer listened to my stammering without cracking a smile. "Best take them back to your rooms, lads," he said. "Right now."

Damn. Arthur and I never got to fire one good shot. Not even one.

On Christmas Eve, the adults gather in the Saloon to enjoy tea with cakes, scones, and sandwiches on the sideboard. The children would have tea in the nursery, but I think the nannies always had trouble getting them to calm down and eat something. William and Harry, along with their cousins, knew that after tea was over they could start opening their presents! In fact, the whole family opens their presents on Christmas Eve, a break from the English tradition of Christmas morning.

While lavish gift giving is what we all would associate with royal life, most of the presents the Windsors give each other are surprisingly modest. I remember hearing a maid say that Her Majesty had been thrilled to receive a covered casserole dish. I couldn't believe it. But the one we all joked about was the annual toilet seat that Prince Charles would receive as a gift—he apparently collects them! Such modest gift giving was limited to the adults; the Windsor children received toys and treats galore. After all, it was Christmas, a fine time to spoil them silly.

A Gift from a Queen

All royal employees get a present each year from Her Majesty, handed over personally. Because there were so many staff, there was a catalog sent round earlier in the year by the Queen's chief housekeeper and you could pick out exactly what you wanted, within a certain price limit, of course. So your annual gift from the Queen wasn't much of a surprise. Some chefs would collect silver or knives and build up collections over the years. Then there were other mischievous chefs who would ask for the most ungainly gifts, like ladders or large stockpots, and grin ear to ear as they watched the Queen struggle to hand it to them.

I understand that now Her Majesty gives everyone the same thing: a Halcyon Days enamel box.

Each year the staff were presented with a (store-bought) Christmas pudding and note card from the Queen.

Feeding the Cooks

It wasn't uncommon to see a fleet of cars heading out of Sandringham after nine at night. With dinner finished we chefs would shower, change, and head out for some local gourmet food. A few miles up the road and along the coast was the Lifeboat Inn. Built four hundred years ago as a smugglers' alehouse, it served the finest moules mariniere I have ever tasted. The mussels came locally from Brancaster and made their short jump from the sea to the frying pan. They were served in a bowl the size of a satellite dish. With a loaf of crusty bread for mopping the juices and a pint of local Abbots ale, five chefs and a kitchen porter were in heaven.

CHRISTMAS DAY

The Windsors, like all families, have their own Christmas traditions that they look forward to year after year. On Christmas Day, they awake to stockings at the foot of their beds, stuffed with small gifts and fruit, and to breakfast being readied for them downstairs. Breakfast isn't too leisurely since the family attends morning services together at St. Mary Magdelenes, located right on Sandringham Estate. There is usually a crowd of well-wishers and media gathered outside the church to see the Queen.

By the time church is over and everyone has returned to the house, Christmas lunch is just about ready. This is the big festive meal of the day. In the dining room, two Christmas trees with colored lights flicker away as the royal family pulls Christmas crackers, reads jokes, and dons paper crowns. Even the Queen wears her paper crown! A large cardboard Santa Claus decorated in red tissue paper is ceremonially perched on the sideboard, its insides stuffed with gifts. The family draws lots to see who gets to pull the first prize from Santa's belly.

Santa on the sideboard

Traditionally the centerpiece of the meal is comprised of large golden roasted turkeys with all the trimmings. These Norfolk birds come from the local butcher, Scoles in Dersingham, along with all the beef, lamb, and pork we served the royal family. The turkeys are served whole and carved right in the dining room by the head chef. We would roast about three twenty-five-pounders on Christmas morning just for the royal table. More turkeys were made for the one hundred staff members we served Christmas lunch. The smell of the roasting birds would fill the whole kitchen and drive us chefs crazy.

To go along with the turkey, there would be sausages wrapped in bacon, brussels sprouts with braised chestnuts, glazed carrots, roasted potatoes, mashed potatoes, cranberry sauce, and don't forget the gravy. A large glass bowl of salad was a must, and sometimes we were lucky enough to serve samphire. Samphire, which is also called saltwort or salicornia, grows in muddy salt marshes by the sea. Picked young and tender, it is pickled to preserve it. It looks a bit like seaweed, but is more like a salty, thin asparagus. You can eat it any time of year, but I always associate it with Christmas at Sandringham.

*Christmas lunch,
Sandringham dining room*

Bread sauce is also a traditional side dish and is as much a part of an English Christmas dinner as stuffing is a part of an American Thanksgiving. Like stuffing, bread sauce was created as a clever way to use up stale bread, but it is quite different in a number of ways. First, it's made with heated milk steeped with onion, cloves, salt, pepper, and bay leaf. Butter and bread crumbs are beaten in to make a thick but still saucy consistency. Bread sauce can't be made very far in advance and is really best served as soon as it's cooked. You spoon it right next to your sliced turkey.

After the main course, there would be dessert, then cheese. Dessert would include two Christmas puddings, brandy sauce, perhaps some warmed mince pie and brandy butter. The cheese board would usually include soft homemade Windsor cheese and a Derby cheese, which is an aged Gloucestershire cheese made with the addition of sage. There would also be a rich double Gloucestershire cheese and a Royal Windsor. A Royal Windsor looks like a large capital *E*, a three-layered cheese whose middle, top, and bottom layers are composed of a port-fortified cheddar, with Stilton filling in the spaces between. We would also set out a huge aged Stilton, which was sent every year from Harrods. It was placed on a large silver tray with a white linen napkin folded around the crust. The top lid was removed and port wine poured over the top of the cheese. Lovely. There was coffee for anyone who wanted, a Higgins dark roast, and chocolate and candies piled high on the sideboard.

After a meal like that it's time for the family to gather round in the Saloon and, like the rest of Great Britain, watch the Queen's brief Christmas broadcast. Afterward Her Majesty would usually take the dogs out for a walk and the rest of the family would either take a good hike in the snow or take a nap. By five o'clock if anyone was hungry—and there were always a few—tea was served on a sideboard laden with chocolate Yule logs, Christmas cake, brandy snaps, mince pies, and sandwiches.

Christmas evening there was always a party swinging in the staff rec hall. As secretary of the Royal Household Social Club (my very official title!), I was usually spinning records or working the bar. All the staff came out to dance and

Christmas Pudding

Thanks to Dickens, plum pudding, also called Christmas pudding, is synonymous with an English Yule. I've always believed that certain sweets and desserts, unlike savory recipes, remain fixed in the collective memory, perennial favorites for centuries. Steamed puddings are a class of old, old English recipes that modern Britain has never abandoned.

During February or March each year we would sterilize the enormous kitchen sink and fill it with dried fruit and raisins that had been macerated in alcohol. Then we would add a bit of flour, sugar, and various spices and peels. The puddings were packed into masonware basins, steamed, cooled, and refrigerated. This "kitchen sink" method would yield about forty puddings. When I was ready to serve it, I would resteam the pudding over a low heat. It would be turned out onto a silver tray and then warm brandy was poured over the pudding and set aflame. The alcohol burns off as the pudding is marched into the royal dining room. Yes, it's a little bit of spectacle, but not just a royal one. It's traditionally English, common and good.

Leftovers for Dinner

Leftovers? For Her Majesty? No, not really. Royal traditions don't include leftover turkey sandwiches. Not yet, at least!

But Christmas dinner was served in a more relaxed buffet style—not a sit-down dinner—and the family was free to taste a wide variety of foods, some very traditional and others more modern. On the classic royal side would be stuffed boars head, boiled beef tongue, smoked turkey, Parma ham, and pâté de foie gras en Croûte. These stood alongside spinach and cream cheese roulades and salmon and vegetable terrines. Minted lamb cutlets and whole sides of poached and decorated salmon were popular too.

have a few drinks. After our hard work, it was our turn to party. And some of us did that with a vengeance. There is nothing like having a heavy head when you have to get up early the next morning for Boxing Day.

Christmas yule logs and a happy birthday cake for Princess Alice, Duchess of Gloucester, the Queen's aunt. Her birthday was Christmas Day.

CLARENCE HOUSE
S.W.1
20th December, 1985

Dear Mr. McGrady,

Queen Elizabeth The Queen Mother bids me write and thank you for your bouquet.

Queen Elizabeth was very touched by your kind thought in presenting Her Majesty with such a lovely bunch of pinks and roses.

The Queen Mother has asked if you would convey an expression of Her Majesty's sincere and grateful thanks to all members of the Royal Household Social Club.

Comptroller to
Queen Elizabeth The Queen Mother

Mr. D. McGrady.

Note thanking me on behalf of the Queen Mum for sending her flowers from the royal household social club.

BOXING DAY

Boxing Day, the day after Christmas, is a uniquely English holiday. There are a number of theories as to why it is called Boxing Day, some involving pugilism! Actually, Boxing Day is also known as St. Stephen's Day and its origins are found in the practice of giving either cash or boxing up gifts for the poor. Traditionally, gifts among equals were exchanged on or before Christmas Day, but gifts for the poor were bestowed the day after.

Today Boxing Day is celebrated as a day of sport. Soccer matches and horse racing are extremely popular ways to spend the day. For the royal family, Boxing Day is always spent shooting. Norfolk's farm landscape is home to all sorts of birds. Partridge, quail, woodcock, wild duck, and pheasant find their way into the royal crosshairs and end up on the royal dinner table. The men start shooting around nine in the morning, and the ladies join them for lunch. Since it is the middle of winter, the cold weather drives everyone indoors and lunch might be set up in one of the stables at Wood Farm. Food is packed in Ascot boxes, transported, and set up on site.

Shooting lunches always looked both rustic and luxurious, a true glimpse of the past. Here we were in this unheated antique barn serving lunch on beautiful silver trays laden with steaming hot food. The shooters have come inside, red cheeked, and are warming up with shots of sloe gin being passed around.

What to Wear

In her memoirs, Sarah, Duchess of York, detailed the changes of clothes required on Christmas Day: tweed skirt and cardigan for breakfast; stylish dress (and coat, hat, and gloves) for church; silk dress for lunch; casual skirt and blouse for the afternoon; silk skirt and blouse for tea; and finally a formal gown for dinner. That is a lot of changing during the day and the duchess clearly thought it was a waste of time. It is easier for her now. The duchess spends Christmas at Wood Farm on the Sandringham estate, where she can see her ex-husband and daughters and also visit with some members of the family in a more relaxed fashion.

Soup was often served to fend off the cold and there might be a selection of small savory pies like chicken and leek pie, chicken curry, or mutton and lamb pies. A warm stew would follow, perhaps a venison and red wine stew or a blanquette de veau. It varied a bit depending upon what the kitchen had on hand. Boulangère or mashed potatoes and sautéed cabbage would be served alongside. After that, and another shot of gin, nobody really minded that the barn was cold. They were plenty warm.

For dessert, we would usually serve a bit of fried plum pudding with brandy butter, treacle tarts, or mince pies. *Treacle* is the English word for molasses. Though to confuse things even more, we don't use treacle in treacle tart; we use golden syrup. Golden syrup is reduced sugar cane syrup the color of honey.

I'd always heard that Sandringham was at its prettiest in July, around the time of the Sandringham flower show. I never saw the estate then, but I can tell you that in winter the landscape was breathtaking, especially when it snowed. After a snowstorm the front of the house looked like a scene from a postcard. Lunch in the barn may have warmed the royals up a bit, but nobody could resist getting back outside. It was so quiet and the cold, clean air and natural beauty of Sandringham put everyone at ease.

No wonder it was Princess Diana's favorite royal residence. She may not have joined in the shooting, but she loved to go for walks in the afternoon all alone "to clear the cobwebs" as she put it. She would walk past Park House and stop to take a look at it. It was a special house to her. After all, it was where she was born.

Wood Farm

Wood Farm was a small farmhouse on the estate, which would accommodate family members from time to time. If the Queen was attending dog trials or the Duke was carriage driving at Sandringham, they would stay at Wood Farm rather than open up the big house. From my perspective as a chef, this was as up close and personal as it got with the royal family. Wood Farm is the size of a regular home and staff was very small with one butler, one chef, one dresser, one footman, one chauffer, and, of course, twelve corgis.

The dining room was right next to the kitchen, and we knew when the Queen was coming through for lunch because the door would open and the dogs would be herded into the kitchen. I could feed as many as twelve in the royal dining room and six in the staff room, all the while navigating around the dogs, which were jumping up for tidbits. You couldn't push the dogs away, for the Queen would hear them yelp in the next room and know what was going on. At the end of the trip the Queen would walk past the kitchen window, wave, and say thank you for a nice weekend. Now *that* is a compliment.

Wood Farm

At Wood Farm, playing with one of Her Majesty's corgis

RINGING IN THE NEW YEAR

New Year's Eve was a bigger party for the staff than for the royal family. Yes, there was a chef on duty to refill the royal mulled wine and canapés, but most everyone else was in the rec hall kicking it up. Everyone, that is, but the footmen. They were

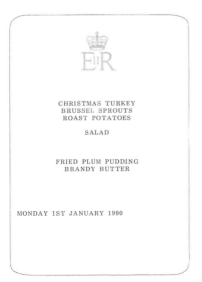

CHRISTMAS TURKEY
BRUSSEL SPROUTS
ROAST POTATOES

SALAD

FRIED PLUM PUDDING
BRANDY BUTTER

MONDAY 1ST JANUARY 1990

*New Year's Day menu
and turkey again*

still on duty, fulfilling an ancient Scottish custom deemed to bring luck for the rest of the year to the house and its inhabitants. This custom dictated that the youngest, darkest-haired footman was to cross the threshold into the house on the stroke of midnight. Once they had completed that ritual, they came over to the rec hall to celebrate the New Year with the rest of us. I remember Cyril Dickman, the palace steward who served more than fifty years with the royal family, stepping up as our official New Year's Eve host. We would all stand in a circle with Cyril in the middle and he would ring a large handbell as we sang "Auld Lang Syne."

Another royal year had come to a close.

STILTON FRITTERS WITH CREAMY WALNUT DRESSING

Fritters

- 1¼ cups water
- 1 stick (8 tablespoons) unsalted butter
- 1 cup all-purpose flour, sifted
- 4 eggs
- ½ cup Stilton cheese, crumbled
- ½ cup grated Gruyère cheese
  Pinch of cayenne pepper
  Salt and freshly ground black pepper
- 4 cups vegetable oil, for frying
- 1 (6-ounce) bag mixed salad leaves
- 1 ripe pear, peeled and sliced
- 1 teaspoon celery seeds

Creamy Walnut Dressing

- ¼ cup olive oil
- 1 teaspoon Dijon mustard
- 1 teaspoon honey
- 1 teaspoon walnuts, about 4 walnut halves
- 1 teaspoon walnut oil
- 1 teaspoon lemon juice
- 1 tablespoon white balsamic vinegar

1. **For the fritters,** put the water and butter in a saucepan, and bring to a boil. The butter should be completely melted before the water boils. Quickly add the sifted flour, and beat with a wooden spoon until the mixture leaves the sides of the pan. Remove the saucepan from the heat. Beat the eggs into the pan, one at a time, beating well after each addition until they are fully incorporated into the flour and butter mixture. While the dough is still warm, beat in the cheeses, cayenne, and salt and pepper to taste.

2. Heat the oil to 325 degrees. Drop the batter by the teaspoon into the oil, and cook each fritter until golden and the cheese is still runny in the middle. Be careful not to crowd the pan by adding too many fritters at once. You will need to do several batches. Drain the cooked fritters on a cooling rack or on a plate lined with paper towels.

3. Arrange the salad leaves and pear slices onto six plates, and sprinkle with the celery seed.

4. **For the Creamy Walnut Dressing**, combine the olive oil, mustard, honey, walnuts, walnut oil, lemon juice, and vinegar in a blender, and taste, adjusting the seasoning if necessary. Drizzle the salad leaves and pear slices with the dressing. Perch 4 or 5 warm fritters on top of each plate and serve immediately.

MAKES 6 SERVINGS

MASHED POTATOES

I spent a whole year at the Savoy Hotel just preparing vegetables. During that time I probably made about ten gallons of mashed potatoes every day. Eventually I fine-tuned a recipe that most say makes amazing mashed potatoes. The secret is in mashing or ricing so there are no lumps, adding plenty of cream and butter and tasting again and again until the seasoning is just perfect. Don't skimp on the butter on the top. The look on everyone's faces as the first person spoons into the potatoes and the melted butter runs into the mash is worth it.

2   pounds red potatoes, peeled and quartered

1/2 stick (4 tablespoons) unsalted butter

1/3 cup heavy cream

2   teaspoons salt, or more to taste

1/8 teaspoon grated nutmeg

1/8 teaspoon ground white pepper

1/2 stick (1/4 cup) salted butter, melted for decoration (optional)

1   tablespoon finely chopped parsley (optional)

1. Place the potatoes in a large pot, add cold water to about 1 inch above the potatoes, cover, and bring to a boil. Lower the heat to a simmer, and cook until the potatoes are tender when pricked with a fork, about 20 minutes.

2. Drain off the water, and put the potatoes in a pan over low heat for 1 to 2 minutes to dry them thoroughly. Mash the potatoes with a potato masher or pass them through a ricer until there are no lumps. Stir in the butter, heavy cream, salt, nutmeg, and white pepper. Adjust the seasoning and place into a serving dish. Flatten the top and garnish with the melted butter and parsley if desired.

MAKES 6 SERVINGS

ROAST TURKEY

1	(14-pound) turkey	2	cups white wine
3	onions, peeled and chopped	3	cups chicken broth
4	carrots, peeled and chopped	1	stick butter, softened
6	ribs celery, chopped	2	tablespoons dried thyme
2	bay leaves		Kosher salt and freshly ground black pepper

1. Remove the turkey from the refrigerator about 1 1/2 hours before cooking to allow it to come to room temperature. Preheat the oven to 325 degrees. Place the onions, carrots, celery, and bay leaves in the bottom of a large roasting pan. Pour the wine and broth over the top.

2. Remove all the giblets inside the turkey. Rinse the turkey thoroughly and pat dry. Rub the softened butter all over the breast and legs of the turkey, and sprinkle all over with the thyme and the salt and pepper. Lay the turkey on its side on top of the vegetables and roast for 1 1/2 hours. Cover with foil if the turkey starts to brown too quickly. Turn the turkey onto its other side, and roast for another hour. Lay the turkey breast side up, remove any foil, and roast until the internal temperature in the thickest part of the thigh registers 170 degrees and the skin is golden brown.

3. Remove the turkey from the oven and place it on a large warmed plate. Tent it with foil to keep the turkey warm and let it rest for 30 minutes. Strain the broth at the bottom of the pan, skim any fat that rises to the top, and use as is, or thicken with all-purpose flour and butter to make a classic turkey gravy.

MAKES 8 SERVINGS

Roast Turkey

BREAD SAUCE

1 large onion, peeled and roughly chopped
2½ cups milk
½ cup heavy cream
6 whole cloves
1 bay leaf
10 to 12 slices white bread, crusts removed
2 tablespoons unsalted butter
Salt and freshly ground pepper

1. Put the onion, milk, cream, cloves, and bay leaf in a large pan, and heat until just below boiling. Turn off the heat and leave the pan for about 30 minutes. Cut the bread into ½-inch dice.

2. Strain the milk mixture into a clean saucepan. Add the bread cubes and butter. Simmer over a low heat stirring occasionally until the mixture starts to thicken. Season with the salt and pepper to taste. Serve in a sauce boat alongside roasted turkey or chicken.

MAKES 8 SERVINGS

PIQUANT DILL AND LIME SAUCE

4 tablespoons unsalted butter, divided
2 cloves garlic, peeled and crushed
½ cup heavy cream
1 tablespoon sugar
2 teaspoons honey
2 teaspoons Dijon mustard
4 tablespoons fresh lime juice
2 tablespoons finely chopped fresh dill

In a small sauté pan over medium heat, melt 2 tablespoons butter. Add the crushed garlic, stir for a minute, and then add the cream, sugar, honey, mustard, and lime juice. Whisk the ingredients together, and increase the heat until the sauce starts to boil. Reduce the liquid by half, or until it gets to a syrup consistency. Remove the pan from the heat, add the remaining 2 tablespoons butter, and shake the pan until the butter blends into the sauce. Stir in the dill. Keep the sauce warm until you are ready to serve it, but do not let it return to a boil.

MAKES 1 CUP OR 4 SERVINGS

CHICKEN AND LEEK PIE

8 ounces pie dough, enough for a 9-inch pie crust

8 ounces frozen puff pastry, thawed

1 stick (8 tablespoons) unsalted butter

1/2 cup all-purpose flour

1 3/4 cups milk

1/2 cup heavy cream

1/4 onion, peeled and left whole

1 bay leaf

Salt and freshly ground pepper

1/2 stick (4 tablespoons) unsalted butter, divided

2 leeks, washed, trimmed, and finely sliced

3 chicken breasts (about 1 pound), skinless and boneless, cut into 1-inch cubes

1/2 teaspoon ground mace

1 tablespoon soy sauce

1 egg, beaten

1. Preheat the oven to 350 degrees. Line a flan ring or pie dish with the pastry dough, weigh it down with pie weights or dried beans, and blind bake (an English term for baking the pastry shell before it is filled) for 15 minutes. Roll out pastry, then cut out a circle of the puff pastry to top the pie, and refrigerate it until ready to use.

2. Melt the stick of butter in a saucepan. Add the flour, and cook the flour in the butter for 1 minute. Slowly add the milk and cream, whisking constantly to eliminate any lumps of flour. Add the onion and bay leaf to the sauce, and season with the salt and pepper to taste. Turn off the heat, cover, and keep warm.

3. Melt 2 tablespoons butter in a separate sauté pan and add the leeks, stirring occasionally until soft and translucent. Remove them to a large bowl. In the same pan add the remaining 2 tablespoons butter and melt over low heat. Season the cubes of chicken with salt and pepper and the mace. Increase the heat to high, and sauté the chicken until it is lightly colored. Remove to a colander to drain off any fat, put the chicken in a bowl with the leeks, and add the soy sauce. Remove the bay leaf and onion from the sauce. Add the leeks, chicken, and sauce together; taste and adjust the seasonings.

4. Spoon the chicken mixture into the partially baked pie shell. Brush the pie crust edges with the beaten egg, and lay the puff pastry lid on top. Brush the puff pastry with the remaining beaten egg, and return the pie to the oven for 30 minutes, or until the pastry is golden brown. Serve hot or cold.

MAKES 6 TO 8 SERVINGS

CURRIED CHICKEN PIES

½   stick (¼ cup) unsalted butter
2   tablespoons mild curry powder
¼   cup all-purpose flour
1   cup chicken broth
½   cup plus 1 tablespoon heavy cream

Salt and freshly ground pepper
1   (2½-pound) roasted chicken, skin and bones removed
1   (17-ounce) box frozen puff pastry, thawed
1   egg, beaten

1. Preheat the oven to 375 degrees. In a sauté pan over high heat, melt the butter and stir in the curry powder. Add the flour and stir until combined. Gradually whisk in the chicken broth and cream, season with the salt and pepper to taste, and reduce the heat to a simmer, for about 5 minutes.

2. Dice the chicken into ¼-inch cubes, and stir into the sauce. Add a little more broth if the sauce is too thick. Heat until bubbling, and adjust the seasoning. Remove from the heat and allow to cool.

3. Roll out both sheets of puff pastry on a lightly floured table into a rectangle about ⅛ inch thick. Using a 2-inch cookie cutter, cut 48 circles out of the dough. Place 1½ teaspoons of the curried chicken filling in the center of half the circles.

4. Brush the other half of the pastry circles with the beaten egg, and press, brushed egg side down, onto the top of the chicken mix, sealing the pastry edges together. Brush the tops of the pies with the remaining beaten egg, and transfer the pies to a baking sheet.

5. Bake in the center of the oven for 15 minutes, or until golden brown. Remove to a cooling rack and allow the pies to cool slightly.

MAKES 24 SMALL PIES

VENISON STEW

2	pounds venison haunch or leg, cut into 1-inch dice		6	juniper berries, crushed
1½	cups red wine		1	teaspoon rosemary
2	medium onions, finely chopped		2	tablespoons olive oil
3	ribs celery, chopped		½	stick (¼ cup) butter
2	carrots, peeled and chopped		½	cup all-purpose flour
1	bay leaf		1¼	cups beef broth
1	teaspoon dried thyme			Salt and freshly ground pepper
4	cloves garlic, crushed		2	tablespoons red currant jelly

1. Marinate the venison, red wine, onions, celery, carrots, bay leaf, thyme, garlic, juniper berries, and rosemary together in a ziplock bag. Seal the bag and refrigerate for up to three days, but at least overnight.

2. Preheat the oven to 350 degrees. Strain the meat, vegetables, and herbs into a colander, reserving the red wine mixture for use later. In a heavy Dutch oven or covered casserole, heat the oil and butter over high heat until the butter melts. Add the meat and vegetables and sauté in batches so not to crowd the pan, until the meat starts to brown. Repeat with all the meat. Set aside all the browned meat and vegetables. In the same pot, add the flour. Stir for several seconds, and then add the beef broth and the reserved red wine mixture from the marinade. Return the venison and vegetables to the pot, and season with the salt and pepper to taste.

3. Bring the sauce to a simmer, cover, and place on the middle oven shelf. Braise for 1½ hours, or until the meat is tender. Remove from the oven, adjust the seasonings, and remove the bay leaf. Stir in the red currant jelly and serve.

MAKES 4 SERVINGS

SUPREME OF PHEASANT STUFFED WITH GOAT CHEESE

4	(5-ounce) pheasant breasts, from 2 (3-pound) young pheasants		Salt and freshly ground black pepper
2	tablespoons unsalted butter	1/4	cup goat cheese, softened
1/2	cup skinned and finely diced red bell pepper	2	tablespoons olive oil
1	pinch dried thyme	1	(14-ounce) package frozen puff pastry, thawed
		1	egg yolk
		2	teaspoons sesame seeds

1. Preheat the oven to 350 degrees. Remove the tenderloin from each pheasant breast, and set the tenderloins aside. Turn each breast skin side down. At a 45-degree angle, make an incision lengthwise on each side of the pheasant breast. This creates a pocket that can be stuffed. Set the breasts aside.

2. Prepare the filling by melting the butter in a small skillet set over medium heat. Add the peppers and sauté until soft and limp. Add the thyme, and season with the salt and pepper. Remove from the heat and cool. Divide the goat cheese and stuff an equal amount in each breast pocket, followed by the red peppers. Lay the reserved tenderloin on top of the filling, and smooth the raised pheasant meat back over the tenderloin, creating a plump, but normal-shaped, pheasant breast. Season the breasts with salt and pepper.

3. Heat the olive oil in the skillet, and sear the breasts for about 2 minutes per side, browning lightly. Remove from the pan to a plate and cool.

4. Open the puff pastry, and roll out to about ¼ inch thick. Cut 8 long strips, approximately 1 x 18 inches, and brush one side of each strip with the egg yolk.

5. Wind the pastry around the pheasant breast, starting at the point and overlapping slightly to cover the pheasant in a spiral cone. The egg-yolk-brushed side of the dough should be facing up, not touching the pheasant breast. You will probably need 2 pieces of the dough to cover each breast, and make sure the pieces are joined on the underside. Sprinkle the sesame seeds on the top, and place breasts on a baking sheet. Chill the pheasants for about 30 minutes. You can prepare up to this stage 12 hours ahead.

6. Bake in the center of the oven for 25 to 30 minutes, or until the pastry is a golden brown. Remove to a plate and let rest in a warm place for 5 minutes. To serve, slice across the breast on the bias to show the filling, and serve with Piquant Dill and Lime Sauce (page 162).

MAKES 4 SERVINGS

LAMB RAAN (INDIAN LEG OF LAMB)

3½ to 4 pounds boneless leg of lamb

6 cloves garlic, crushed

1 onion, finely diced

2 tablespoons olive oil

1 cup plain yogurt

1 teaspoon salt

½ cup ground raw cashew nuts

1 tablespoon garam masala

1 tablespoon fresh ginger, crushed

2 tablespoons red chili sauce (Sriracha or other chile garlic sauce)

1 teaspoon ground cumin

½ cup chopped fresh mint

1. Rinse and pat dry the leg of lamb. Score the lamb, cutting ½ inch deep into the skin about 6 to 8 times. Place the garlic, onion, olive oil, yogurt, salt, cashew nuts, garam masala, crushed ginger, chili sauce, and cumin into a large ziplock bag, and mix well. Add the lamb, rubbing the marinade into the lamb, especially into the cut areas. Refrigerate for at least two hours and up to two days. The flavor will get stronger the longer the lamb marinates.

2. Preheat the oven to 350 degrees. Remove the lamb from the bag onto a roasting pan, and pour the marinade over the top. Bake for 2 hours, or until the lamb is tender. Baste with the juices several times during cooking.

3. Remove the lamb from the roasting pan, and allow to rest for about 15 minutes. Reduce the remaining meat juices/marinade to a sauce consistency. Slice the lamb into ½-inch-thick slices, pour the sauce over the slices, and garnish with the chopped mint.

MAKES 6 TO 8 SERVINGS

NAVARIN OF LAMB WITH HERBED DUMPLINGS

Lamb

- 3 pounds leg of lamb, cubed
  Salt and freshly ground pepper
- 1/4 cup olive oil
- 1/2 stick butter
- 8 cloves garlic, chopped
- 1 large onion, chopped
- 3 large carrots, chopped
- 4 ribs celery, chopped
- 1 large leek, white parts only, cleaned and chopped
- 1/2 cup flour
- 1/4 cup tomato paste
- 1 bay leaf
- 1 tablespoon Worcestershire sauce
- 2 quarts beef broth

Dumplings

- 3 cups all-purpose flour
- 8 teaspoons baking powder
- 1 teaspoon salt
- 1 1/3 cups milk
- 1 teaspoon Dijon mustard
- 4 eggs
- 3 tablespoons chopped fresh chives
- 4 tablespoons chopped fresh parsley
  Chopped fresh parsley for garnish
  Salt and freshly ground pepper

1. Preheat the oven to 350 degrees.

2. **For the lamb,** season the lamb with the salt and pepper. Heat the oil until hot, but not smoking, in a heavy, covered casserole or Dutch oven. Fry the lamb cubes until brown, and then remove them to a bowl. Drain the oil from the casserole. Return the pot to the heat, and add the butter. When melted, sauté the garlic, onion, carrots, celery, and leek until limp. Stir in the flour, tomato paste, bay leaf, and Worcestershire sauce. Gradually add the beef broth, stirring continuously, and return the cubed lamb to the pot. Bring to a simmer, cover with a lid, and place the lamb in the oven for 2 hours, or until the meat is tender. Remove the Navarin from the oven, and taste and correct the seasoning. Remove bay leaf.

3. **For the dumplings,** in a large bowl add the flour, baking powder, and salt, and whisk until mixed. In a small bowl add the milk and mustard, and beat in the eggs. Add the herbs. Stir the wet mixture into the flour mixture and combine. Divide the dough into 6 to 8 balls. Ladle the Navarin lamb into a casserole or Pyrex dish. Drop the dumplings evenly over the lamb, and return the entire stew to the oven for an additional 20 minutes, or until the dumplings have puffed up and cooked through. Sprinkle with the chopped parsley and serve.

MAKES 6 TO 8 SERVINGS

A shooting lunch: Steamed Syrup Sponge Pudding (top left),
Curried Chicken Pies (top right), Mashed Potatoes (bottom left),
Navarin of Lamb

IRISH STEW

¼	cup olive oil
2	pounds lamb leg, cut into 2-inch chunks
4	medium potatoes, peeled and cubed into 1½-inch pieces
3	large carrots, peeled and chopped
3	medium onions, chopped

	Salt and freshly ground pepper
2	teaspoons dried thyme
1	cube beef bouillon
1	cube chicken bouillon
2	bay leaves
1	quart water or less
½	cup chopped fresh parsley

1. Heat the oil in a large sauté pan until hot, but not smoking. Sear the lamb until brown, and set the meat aside in a bowl. Drain off all but a thin layer of oil. Layer the potatoes, carrots, onions, and lamb in a Dutch oven or enameled covered casserole. Add salt and pepper to taste, the thyme, bouillon cubes, and the bay leaves on top. Add just enough water to cover the meat and vegetables.

2. Heat the casserole on high until the liquid just comes to a boil. Cover and reduce the heat to simmer. Cook the stew for 2½ hours, or until the meat is tender. When done, remove from the heat, skim off the top layer of fat, and adjust the seasonings. Remove the bay leaves, and sprinkle with the parsley.

3. Serve hot with lots of soda bread to mop up the juices. This dish is even better reheated the next day.

MAKES 6 SERVINGS

BREAST OF PHEASANT WITH A PEARL BARLEY "RISOTTO"

The earthy flavors really come through in this dish. But don't worry if you can't get pheasant or are not keen on game; chicken breasts are a fine substitute. It's worth paying a little extra for the chanterelle mushrooms. And if your wallet allows, a few morel mushrooms would be wonderful.

2	pheasant breasts, or 2 (5-ounce) chicken breasts
1	tablespoon olive oil
8	sprigs fresh or 1⅛ teaspoon dried savory
1	lemon, zest and juice only
1	cup pearl barley
2	cups cold water
1	tablespoon butter

4	slices (4 ounces) smoked bacon, cut into lardoons
2	small leeks, washed and finely chopped
6	ounces chanterelles or button mushrooms, cut into bite-size pieces
2	cups chicken broth
6	ounces goat cheese, softened
	Salt and freshly ground pepper

1. Marinate the pheasant breasts with the olive oil, lemon juice, and 2 sprigs (or ⅛ teaspoon dried) savory in a ziplock bag in the refrigerator for at least 1 hour, or up to 24 hours. Before grilling, remove the pheasant breasts from the refrigerator and allow them to come to room temperature.

2. Bring the pearl barley and water to a boil in a heavy pan, and simmer over low heat for 20 minutes, or until the liquid has evaporated and the barley is tender. In a large pan, melt the butter and sauté the bacon until it starts to crisp. Add the leeks and mushrooms and cook over a medium heat until softened.

3. Preheat the grill to medium hot. Sear the pheasant breasts, or chicken breasts, on the grill over direct heat about 4 to 6 minutes per side, or until they reach preferred doneness. I like to serve the pheasant pink. Set each breast on a clean plate to rest for 5 minutes.

4. Stir the pearl barley and chicken broth into the bacon and mushroom mixture, and simmer until the liquid starts to appear like a shiny glaze. Fold in the goat cheese, 6 sprigs fresh (or 1 teaspoon dried) savory, and lemon zest. Add the salt and pepper to taste.

5. Spoon the barley risotto onto plates next to the pheasant.

MAKES 2 SERVINGS

BEEF CURRY — ENGLISH STYLE

When Queen Victoria was on the throne and Britain still had an empire, there were two Indian chefs employed in the royal kitchens whose sole job was to make a curry every day for the royal table. Now whenever curry is on the menu, often for shooting lunches, it is prepared by the chef/saucier on duty. This recipe makes a mild curry; the Queen isn't fond of very spicy food. It uses curry powder developed for the British palate, which includes coriander, turmeric, cumin, fenugreek, ginger, garlic, fennel seed, cardamom, nutmeg, red pepper, and cinnamon. Feel free to use any curry powder you like, hot or mild.

2	tablespoons olive oil
1½	pounds beef chuck or round, cut into 1-inch cubes
1	large onion, chopped
2	cloves garlic, chopped
¼	cup curry powder
¼	cup all-purpose flour

1	tablespoon tomato paste
3	cups water
3	beef bouillon cubes
1	apple, peeled and chopped
1	tablespoon mango chutney
	Salt and ground black pepper

1. Heat the oil in a Dutch oven able to accommodate all the ingredients. When the oil is hot, add the beef cubes, and brown. Remove the beef. Strain off any excess fat in the bottom of the pot, leaving about 1 to 2 tablespoons. Return the pot to the stove, add the onions and garlic, and sauté until the onions start to soften. Stir in the curry powder and return the beef cubes to the pot. Stir in the flour and tomato paste. Gradually add the water and the bouillon cubes and keep stirring.

2. Add the chopped apple, place a lid on the pot and simmer, either on top of the stove or in a 325 degrees oven for 1 hour, or until the meat is fork tender. Add the mango chutney to taste and season with the salt and pepper. Serve with basmati rice pilaf and pappadams.

MAKES 4 SERVINGS

BASMATI RICE PILAF

2	cups chicken broth		1	tablespoon butter
1	tablespoon olive oil		1/2	cup sliced almonds
1/2	onion, finely diced			Salt and freshly ground pepper
1	cup basmati rice		2	tablespoons chopped fresh cilantro

1. In a small saucepan, bring the chicken broth to a boil. In a separate heavy saucepan, heat the olive oil until warm, add the onion, and sauté until it starts to soften. Stir in the rice. Add the hot chicken broth and stir. Bring the rice to a boil, and then reduce the heat to a simmer. Cover and cook for 18 minutes, or until all of the liquid has evaporated.

2. In a frying pan, melt the butter and add the almonds. Cook until they are golden brown. Transfer the cooked rice into a large bowl, fluff up the grains with a fork and add salt and pepper. Pour the butter and almonds over the rice and garnish with the chopped cilantro.

MAKES 4 SERVINGS

MINCE PIES

Filling

3	cups apple, peeled, cored, and diced
1/2	cup mixed candied peel
2	cups raisins
1	cup currants
1	cup grated beef suet
1	lemon, juice and zest only
1	orange, juice and zest only
1	cup Demerara sugar
1/2	teaspoon ground nutmeg
1/2	teaspoon ground cloves
1	teaspoon ground cinnamon
1/2	cup brandy
1/2	cup port wine

Assembly

2	boxes frozen puff pastry, thawed
1	egg, beaten
2	tablespoons powdered sugar

1. **For the filling**, place the apples, candied peel, raisins, currants, suet, lemon juice and zest, orange juice and zest, sugar, nutmeg, cloves, cinnamon, brandy, and port wine in a large bowl and stir. Refrigerate in a plastic container with a tight-fitting lid for at least three weeks before using. Any leftover mincemeat can be kept for up to a year in the refrigerator.

2. Preheat the oven to 350 degrees.

3. **For the assembly,** roll out the puff pastry on a lightly floured table to about 1/8 inch thick, and cut out 48 (2-inch) circles using a cookie cutter. Place about 1 1/2 teaspoons of mincemeat filling in half the circles. Brush the remaining 24 circles with the beaten egg. Press, egg side down, onto the top of the mincemeat, sealing the pastry edges together. Brush the tops of the pies with the beaten egg, and transfer to a baking sheet.

4. Bake in the center of the oven for 15 minutes, or until golden brown. Remove to a cooling rack and allow the pies to cool slightly. Dust with the powdered sugar before serving.

MAKES 24 SMALL INDIVIDUAL PIES

TREACLE TART

This tart is traditional British comfort food dating back to the seventeenth century when it was made using treacle, *the English word for molasses. Most people now use golden syrup, a product made by evaporating sugar cane juice to the consistency of corn syrup. It has a nutty taste without the bitterness of molasses. It is Harry Potter's favorite dessert and "Harry Wales" enjoyed it too.*

3/4 cup plus 2 tablespoons unsalted butter, softened	3 1/2 cups all-purpose flour
3/4 cup plus 2 tablespoons granulated sugar	1 (1-pound) jar golden syrup
1 egg	2 cups (about 7 slices) fresh white bread crumbs, without crusts
1 teaspoon vanilla paste	1 lemon, juiced

1. Preheat the oven to 350 degrees. Cream the butter and sugar until light in color. Add the egg and vanilla paste, and slowly incorporate the flour to form a ball. Wrap this dough in parchment paper or plastic wrap, and refrigerate for at least 1 hour before using. This will make more pastry than you need for a single tart, but I always like to have some spare dough in the refrigerator. It keeps for at least three weeks.

2. Roll out the dough to about 1/2 inch thick, and line an 8-inch flan ring or pie dish. Chill until ready to fill. In a large bowl, combine the golden syrup, bread crumbs, and lemon juice, and spoon the mixture into the pie shell.

3. Bake in the center of the oven for 30 minutes, or until the pastry edges are golden brown. Remove from the oven, and allow to cool slightly. Slice and serve with ice cream, whipped cream, or English custard.

MAKES 6 SERVINGS

A note in the menu book from the Queen, requesting treacle tart

CHOCOLATE ROULADE "YULE LOG"

An English custom dating from the twelfth century dictates that on Christmas Eve an enormous log of freshly cut wood be brought into the house. This "Yule Log" would be placed on the hearth and sprinkled with mulled wine, oil, and salt. Prayers would be said and the log would be lit. It was believed that the log's cinders would protect the house from lightning and from the devil's power.

Over the years the log became smaller and was transformed into a centerpiece on the Christmas table, decorated with candles and greenery. Eventually in some homes the wood disappeared entirely and was replaced with a chocolate cake in the shape of a log. That is the tradition with the royal family, where each Christmas Eve I would prepare a Yule Log for the royal table.

Filling

- 1¼ cups heavy cream
- 8 ounces bittersweet chocolate, melted

Roulade

- 2 tablespoons butter, for greasing tray
- 2 tablespoons all-purpose flour, for dusting tray
- 8 eggs, separated
- 1¾ cups granulated sugar, divided
- ¾ cup potato starch
- ½ cup Dutch processed cocoa powder

Frosting

- 2½ cups heavy cream
- 1 pound semisweet or bittersweet chocolate, melted

  Grated chocolate, for garnish

  Powdered sugar, for garnish

1. **For the filling**, a day ahead bring the cream to the boil, and pour it onto the 8 ounces melted chocolate, whisking all the time until the cream is mixed into the chocolate. Leave to cool at room temperature overnight.

2. **For the roulade**, preheat the oven to 350 degrees. Line an 18 x 12-inch baking sheet with parchment paper. Grease the parchment and lightly dust with flour. In a mixing bowl whisk the egg yolks and 1½ cups sugar until pale. Sift the potato starch and cocoa together into a bowl. Whip the egg whites until stiff and fold half the egg whites into the egg yolks and sugar mixture. Then fold in the potato starch and cocoa mix. Finally fold in the remaining half of the whipped whites.

3. Spread the sponge mixture onto the parchment-prepared tray, and bake in the center of the oven for 15 minutes, or until the sponge is firm to touch in the center.

4. Remove from the oven and loosen the edges of the sponge with a sharp knife. Place an 18 x 12-inch piece of the second parchment paper on a table or counter and sprinkle with the remaining ¼ cup sugar. Invert the sponge onto the sugared parchment paper and allow to cool.

5. Spread the filling over the sponge, leaving a ½-inch edge unfilled around all four sides. Holding the parchment paper, roll the sponge up like a jelly roll. Lift the roll onto a large cooling rack with a tray underneath.

6. Measure 4 inches from the end of the roll and cut a piece off at an angle. Do the same on the other end, starting to cut 2 inches from the top this time. Use some of the filling to stick the two pieces onto the roll. I put the 4-inch piece on the side in the middle of the large roll and the 2-inch piece on the top to create a "chopped log" effect.

7. For the frosting, bring the cream to the boil, and pour it on the melted chocolate in a large bowl, whisking all the time until the cream is mixed in. Ladle the chocolate frosting over the top and sides of the log, covering all of the sponge. Leave until set, about four hours, and then decorate with the grated chocolate and powdered sugar.

MAKES 8 SERVINGS

TRADITIONAL IRISH SODA BREAD

4	cups all-purpose flour	1	teaspoon kosher salt
1	teaspoon baking soda	1¾	cups buttermilk

1. Preheat the oven to 425 degrees. Sift the flour, baking soda, and salt into a large mixing bowl. Gradually add the buttermilk, stirring gently, and binding the dry ingredients together with the buttermilk to form a large round of dough. Place the dough on a lightly greased baking sheet, and make a cross about 1 inch deep on top of the dough.

2. Cover the soda bread dough with something like a large cake pan and bake for about 30 minutes. Remove the cake pan to brown the bread, and bake for 10 more minutes. The bread, when fully baked, will have a hollow sound when tapped on the bottom.

MAKES 6 SERVINGS

CHRISTMAS CAKE

Christmas cakes were one of the first things on our minds once the court moved back to Buckingham Palace from Balmoral Castle. We needed about three months to let the cakes mature, and we would "feed" them every week with syrup. If you plan to make this recipe for Christmas, you'll need to start baking in September.

2 1/2 cups currants

2 1/2 cups sultanas

3/4 cup brandy

1 cup glacé cherries, quartered

1 orange, zest and juice only

1 large lemon, zest and juice only

4 sticks (1 pound) unsalted butter, softened

1/2 cup plus 1 tablespoon unsulfured molasses

2 1/4 cups Muscovado or turbinado sugar

8 eggs, lightly beaten

3 cups all-purpose flour

3 tablespoons brandy

1/2 cup sugar

1/2 cup water

1/2 (12-ounce) jar apricot jam

1 cup powdered sugar

1 1/2 pounds marzipan

1 tablespoon brandy

1 1/2 pounds ready-to-roll fondant icing

1. The day before preparing, mix the currants, sultanas, brandy, cherries, and orange and lemon zest and juices in a large bowl, and let them steep overnight.

2. Preheat the oven to 325 degrees. Line a 10-inch cake pan with parchment paper on the bottom and sides.

3. Cream the butter, molasses, and sugar until light and fluffy. Gradually add the eggs and flour, alternating until both are incorporated. Gradually stir the mixed fruit into the cake mix until combined, and spoon into the prepared tin. Bake in the center of the oven for about 2 1/2 hours. If the top starts to brown, place a sheet of aluminum foil over the cake until it is cooked. The cake is ready when a skewer inserted into the center of the cake comes out clean.

4. Remove the cake to a cooling rack and leave in the pan until cold. Remove the cake and wrap it first in parchment paper and then in plastic wrap. Leave in a cool, dry place for three months, brushing it once a week with a solution of 3 tablespoons brandy mixed with 5 tablespoons sugar syrup (1/2 cup sugar dissolved in 1/2 cup water).

5. To finish the cake, heat the apricot jam, pass through a sieve, and liberally brush it over the cake. Unwrap the cake, and place it upright on a cake dish. In a little powdered sugar, roll out the marzipan about 1/8 inch thick into a circle big enough to cover the top and sides of the cake. Drape the marzipan over the cake as smoothly as possible. Trim any excess at the base. Then roll out the fondant dough in a little powdered sugar into a circle big enough to cover the top and sides of the cake. Cover the cake, smoothing out the top and sides. The cake will keep for up to four weeks.

MAKES 10 SERVINGS

MULLED WINE

1	bottle red wine	1	apple, halved and sliced, core removed
3	tablespoons Muscovado sugar		
1	cup granulated sugar	1	bay leaf
1	cinnamon stick	4	whole cloves
1/2	teaspoon grated nutmeg	1	cup brandy
1	orange, halved and sliced	1	cup port wine
1	lemon, halved and sliced	1	cup freshly squeezed orange juice

Pour the wine, sugars, cinnamon, nutmeg, orange and lemon and apple slices, bay leaf, cloves, brandy, port wine, and orange juice into a stainless steel pan, and place over a low heat until just warm. Do not boil or you will burn off the alcohol. Strain into glasses and serve.

MAKES 2 QUARTS

BRANDY SAUCE

1/2	stick (1/4 cup) unsalted butter	1 1/2	cups heavy cream
1/2	cup all-purpose flour	1/3	cup sugar
1 1/4	cups milk	1/4	cup brandy

In a heavy saucepan set over a high heat, melt the butter, and stir in the flour until combined. Gradually whisk in the milk and cream until combined and reduce the heat to low. Simmer for about 10 minutes, remove from the heat, and whisk in the sugar and brandy.

MAKES 6 SERVINGS

CHRISTMAS PUDDING

We would make ten times this recipe each October after returning from Balmoral. The puddings would then be ready to use the next year (prep time is 3 months to 2 years). These would be sent to Balmoral and Sandringham for shooting and hunting lunches. For shooting lunches we would cut fingers of pudding 3 x 1¼ inches and fry both sides in clarified butter until warm. Hunters would get two fingers of cold pudding in their sack lunches.

Like the recipe for mincemeat, Christmas pudding includes beef suet, which is the very fine white fat surrounding the kidneys. It isn't always easy to find, so ask your local independent butcher and they'll usually know where to get some.

½ stick (¼ cup) unsalted butter, plus butter for greasing	3½ tablespoons pumpkin pie spice
5 cups raisins	3 eggs
3 cups currants	2 cups Demerara sugar
2 cups candied lemon peel	2 cups dark beer
2½ cups grated beef suet	½ cup dark rum
6 cups fresh white bread crumbs	½ cup brandy, plus ¼ cup brandy, for pouring
1¼ cups all-purpose flour	

1. Using a pastry brush, lightly grease the bottom and sides of the pudding bowls and also three square pieces of parchment large enough to cover the tops of the bowls.

2. Mix together in a large bowl the butter, raisins, currants, lemon peel, suet, bread crumbs, flour, pie spice, eggs, sugar, beer, rum, and ½ cup brandy; divide the mixture equally among the pudding bowls. Place the parchment paper on top of the bowls, and cover each with aluminum foil, wrapping tightly around the bowl.

3. Put the pudding bowls in a large steamer with a lid, making sure the water comes at least halfway up the sides of the bowls. Boil for 5 hours, checking the water in the steamer every hour. You will probably need to add more water.

4. Remove the bowls from the steamer and allow the puddings to cool. Refrigerate for *at least* three months and up to two years.

5. To serve, reheat the pudding in a steamer for 2 hours. Invert onto a warm dinner plate. Warm the remaining ¼ cup brandy, pour it over the pudding, and set alight. Serve immediately with brandy sauce (page 179).

MAKES THREE 2-POUND PUDDING BOWLS

STEAMED SYRUP SPONGE PUDDING

Recipes for steamed puddings are legion in British cookbooks, especially old cookbooks. They are usually easy to assemble, stovetop friendly, and always delicious. This pudding can be steamed in two ways. You can steam it in a double boiler fitted with a steamer insert and a well-fitting lid, or you can place the pudding basin on a rack laid inside a pot. If you choose the latter, the water inside the pot should come halfway up the sides of the pudding basin. With either method, check your water levels from time to time. You don't want the double boiler or the pot running dry.

1 stick (1/2 cup) unsalted butter, softened, plus butter for greasing	1 teaspoon vanilla paste
3/4 cup granulated sugar	1 1/2 cups self-rising flour
2 eggs	1 lemon, zest and juice only, divided
1 egg yolk	3 tablespoons milk
	2 cups golden syrup, divided

1. Lightly grease a two-pint pudding basin and a piece of parchment paper large enough to fit over the top of the basin.

2. In a large bowl cream the butter and sugar, and gradually add the eggs, egg yolk, and vanilla paste. Then fold in the flour, followed by the lemon zest, milk, and finally the lemon juice.

3. Place 1 cup golden syrup into the bottom of the prepared pudding basin, and gently spoon the sponge pudding mixture on top. Cover with the parchment paper and a piece of foil, and fold the edges tightly over the basin. Carefully place the pudding into the steamer, or on a rack in a pot, and steam for about 1 1/2 to 2 hours. Check the water level in the steamer/double boiler after the first hour, and add more water if necessary.

4. To serve, remove the foil and parchment paper, and loosen the pudding around the edges of the basin with a sharp knife or offset spatula. Invert the pudding onto a warmed plate, and pour the remaining 1 cup golden syrup over the top. Serve with English custard, ice cream, or whipped cream.

MAKES 6 SERVINGS

TRADITIONAL ENGLISH TRIFLE

1   (11-ounce) Sara Lee all-butter pound cake

1   cup raspberry jam, or half a 12-ounce jar

1   cup fresh raspberries

1 1/3   cups granulated sugar, divided

1 1/4   cups water

4   tablespoons sherry (optional)

2   cups heavy cream

5   egg yolks

1/2   teaspoon vanilla paste

2   teaspoons cornstarch

1 1/4   cups heavy cream, whipped to soft peaks for topping

1   Cadbury's chocolate flake or 2 ounces milk chocolate for garnish

1. Cut the pound cake into 3/4-inch slices, and sandwich the cake slices together with a lavish layer of raspberry jam. Lay the cake sandwiches into a large glass bowl across the bottom in a single layer and slightly up the sides. Spread the fresh raspberries on top. Boil 1 cup sugar and the water together in a small saucepan for 5 minutes, or until the sugar melts and forms a light syrup. Add the sherry, if using, to the syrup, and pour the warm syrup over the pound cake and berries.

2. Bring the heavy cream to a boil in a large saucepan. In a separate bowl, mix the egg yolks, 1/3 cup sugar, vanilla paste, and cornstarch together in a small bowl. Pour the hot cream over the egg mixture, whisking all the while until all the cream is added. Return the cream and egg mixture to the saucepan and continue to stir over low heat until it just starts to thicken. Don't overcook. Remove from the heat, and allow the cream to cool slightly before pouring over the sponge.

3. Refrigerate the trifle until the custard has chilled and set. To serve, spoon the whipped cream over the top of the custard. Decorate with the chocolate flake or grated chocolate.

MAKES 6 TO 8 SERVINGS
OR 4 SERVINGS IF YOU LIVE IN MY HOUSE

(left to right) Mince Pies, Chocolate Roulade "Yule Log," Traditional English Trifle

CHAPTER SEVEN

Kensington Palace

A Home for All Seasons

Kensington Palace was the last place I worked in England and in some ways was the most important place I have ever worked. It was the residence of Princess Diana until her death and it was the place she turned into a home for herself and her sons, William and Harry.

I remember cooking at Wood Farm for Her Majesty one December day in 1992, while she attended the dog trials. She had just returned after the event and sat in her Land Rover, listening to Prime Minister John Major tell the House of Commons—and the rest of the world—that the Prince and Princess of Wales were to separate. I have never shaken that image of the Queen, alone in her car, quietly listening to the radio. It was a sad moment for us all, but especially for her. It had only been a few weeks since the great fire at Windsor Castle—and now this. I immediately thought that I would no longer see Princess Diana at any of the royal houses and might not see too much of the boys either.

But things turned out differently than I thought. It was Prince Charles who moved out of Kensington Palace. Princess Diana stayed and the staff that had served them both was split accordingly. Prince Charles took two of the chefs and left one with the princess, creating a vacancy. I decided to throw my hat in the ring. I got word to the princess that I wanted the position and my interest must have been well received. All other applicants were dropped and the subsequent interview was a mere formality.

I went to work for the princess for the next four years. It wasn't that long really, but my memories of those years are so full that they tend to crowd out the years spent working at Buckingham Palace. Sure, I was sorry to leave my kitchen mates and traveling around the world in "royal style" with Her Majesty, but otherwise I was ready to go. I had worked my way up from junior cook to senior pastry chef and was now ready for a new challenge. At Kensington I would be responsible for running a whole (albeit small) kitchen, a refreshing change from the more rigid partie system at the palace.

Happy Di-ner

■ A SIGH of hungry relief from the Princess of Wales who has been missing the snacks so tenderly prepared by her Kensington Palace chef, Darren McGrady: he has been away for three weeks convalescing at his parents' home in Newark, Nottinghamshire, following a hernia operation.

But now divorce Darren, 33, who was moved from Buckingham Palace to KP at Diana's request, is back in the kitchen serving up the Princess's favourite dishes — she once said he made the best bread and butter pudding in the world.

'She's very happy he's back; they get on very well together,' says a chum. 'And his return is very timely. Diana wants to get moving on holding a few dinner parties.'

My return to the Kensington was picked up by the press

Even though I knew Princess Diana from the palace, my relationship with her really took off when I started working at Kensington. She was entering a new stage in her life and taking better care of herself. Her years as a bulimia sufferer had ended and she was eating properly. She had willpower. I often teased her when I made donuts for the boys, saying, "Go on, your Royal Highness, try one."

"Oh, Darren," she would reply, "that will go straight to my hips." And she would grab a piece of fruit instead.

The Kensington apartment was elegant and comfortable, laid out over three floors with a nursery for the boys. There was a small open kitchen that was a pleasure for me to work in, especially after the labyrinthine kitchens of Windsor or Buckingham Palace. The kitchen had a huge window that opened onto a courtyard. There was no room there for me to grow anything, so I had a window box built and began cultivating fresh herbs. On warm days, all of the windows in the courtyard would be open and the princess's favorite opera arias would waft into the kitchen. I think it might have made my herbs grow a bit faster!

The apartment's location was perfect for Princess Diana. Situated right in the heart of London near Chelsea and Notting Hill, Kensington put the princess in the midst of busy city life. She could pop off down the road and stop into her favorite café for a cappuccino or call in on one of her girlfriends. Shopping was nearby and she could get around London easily.

Everything about life at Kensington was more relaxed than life with the royal family. When William and Harry were at home with their mum, the rules of etiquette were eased. In fact, there was quite a bit of huffing and puffing from the nanny who thought it scandalous that the boys were eating their dinners with their mum off of trays while watching a video. Even when lunch was served in the dining room, the princess and the boys ate family-style. Food was served "all in," which meant both courses were placed on the sideboard before they entered the dining room.

This style of service, sometimes used by the Queen, gave more privacy and meant the butlers didn't have to keep coming in and out of the dining room. The princess would usually tuck into a piece of chicken and a salad, while the boys would have chicken, roasted potatoes, and some vegetables. I would occasionally roast potatoes for the princess too, though unlike the boys, she would have the fat-free version. For that I'd toss the potatoes in egg whites, salt, and paprika and bake. Dessert was usually something like banana flan and the princess might skip that in favor of a yogurt. What a change from Buckingham Palace. Now everyone just passed food round the table and chatted up a storm. It was exactly what the princess wanted for her boys.

It was a simpler household too. When I came to Kensington, Princess Diana had a household staff of twelve. There were two chefs, two butlers, two dressers, a police protection officer, two housemaids, a kitchen helper, a chauffeur, and a nanny. It soon became clear that was too many. The princess began eliminating some positions but kept her favorite staff, those she felt she could trust.

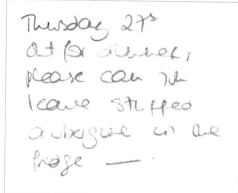

Instructions from "the boss"

By the time she died, the number had whittled down to just five: a chef, butler, nanny, housemaid, and kitchen maid, and a part-time housekeeper. It was a small group and the typical royal household divisions melted away. If the princess's car needed gas—here were the keys. Someone knocking at the door or ringing on the phone? Go and answer it. The role of chef expanded to become that of a caretaker for the princess and the boys when they were home.

My cooking reflected this new environment. No more traditional French cuisine with demi glace and cream reductions and certainly no pheasant, grouse, or deer.

A Princess in the Kitchen

Great news. I can head out early to see Wendy.

Soon after coming to work for Princess Diana, I began dating Wendy, who is now my wife. The princess quickly figured out that the relationship was serious, so she would urge me to leave early on Friday to get a jumpstart on the weekend. I would leave food ready to be microwaved—nothing fancy—and make sure there was plenty for Her Royal Highness to choose from. That was important. The princess did many things, but cooking was not one of them.

Once she tried to cook dinner for a girlfriend. She decided to make an easy pasta dish and she must have let the pasta water boil over. The gas pilot light blew out and by Sunday morning, the princess could smell gas. She called security and they immediately sent out a call to the local firehouse. When I came back on Monday, the princess gleefully informed me that she had twelve hunky men in her house while I was gone. When I heard the whole story, I just laughed. The princess did too.

Darren, can you give this to Wendy, please?" the princess said as she presented me with an envelope one Christmas Eve.

In fact, *game* referred exclusively to the boys' PlayStation! If I was cooking only for the princess, breakfast was sure to be freshly squeezed juices, yogurt, maybe some scrambled eggs, or that quintessential British invention, beans on toast. That had zero fat, but loads of carbs to give Her Royal Highness energy at the gym.

For lunch or dinner, Princess Diana loved pasta, fresh vegetables, chicken, and fish. If she was home alone for lunch, she would have a place set at the kitchen counter. She would wander in around one, and I would serve her lunch and salad on her favorite Herrand Rothschild bird china. Dessert was always fruit or yogurt. Lychees were her all-time favorite. She could work through a pound of them without even thinking. When they were in season, I'd leave a bowl of them out in the sitting room for her.

The boys were easy to feed as well. They had typical childhood favorites, all the things my own children now enjoy—like stuffed potato skins, roasted chicken, pizza, and pasta. They were even pretty good about eating their veggies. Nanny made sure of that. The entire family loved ice cream, and often either William or Harry would wander into the kitchen looking for his favorite Haagen-Dazs chocolate chocolate chip. They were always polite enough to ask, and then helped themselves to a spoon and the ice cream. William would sit in the kitchen windowsill, his spoon digging right into the container, chatting away and keeping one eye on the stairs for Nanny.

You didn't get that at Buckingham Palace. If the boys were visiting Granny and wanted ice cream, the Queen would call her page, who in turn would call the head chef. The head chef would call the pastry kitchen and the pastry chef would in turn call the silver pantry for some silver dishes to present it on. The ice cream would be formed into decorative quenelle shapes and placed in the silver dessert dish. Then it was off to the linen room to get the proper napkin.

The boys' lunch: (left to right) Corn on the Cob, Banana Flan, Roast Pork, Potato Skins

Eventually a footman would arrive to take the ice cream up to the royal dining room some fifteen minutes later.

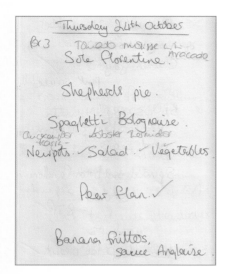

The cousins, Fergie's daughters, often came over for a visit when they were in town, much to William and Harry's delight. They would all run about the house shrieking at the top of their lungs and enjoying themselves immensely. The Duchess of York would stay for tea and visit. The princess adored the girls and would make sure they each had a gift and that a balloon was tied to each child's chair. Tea would include several kinds of sandwiches, one being jam pennies—the Queen's favorite. Chocolate chip cookies were a must since all the children loved them, and the princess realized that children need sweets too, from time to time.

I tried to keep the cooking healthy for everyone, but occasionally met with resistance from the household's younger members. One afternoon I entered the kitchen to see a hand-written note on the counter that read: "Darren, please give the boys pizza tonight. Thank you." It was signed by the nanny, but something about the crooked eight-year-old handwriting gave it away as the work of Prince Harry. I prepared roasted chicken and vegetables and sent it all up with a private chuckle.

Harry bounded into the kitchen the next day telling me he was going to get his mother to allow pizza for dinner that night. I dangled the note in front of him

Junior Apprentices

William and Harry came by the kitchen fairly often looking for a treat or to find out what was for dinner or even just to grab a piece of fruit. But every once in a while they would try their hand at cooking. "Can we help make Mummy's dinner, please?" they would ask. The princess's favorite dish was stuffed eggplant and the boys would get very excited about putting that together. No matter that it looked like smashed eggplant when it was done, they served it proudly and the princess was thrilled. She would eat every bite. I'm sure it tasted delicious—it was made with such love.

and asked, "Do you think I should let the nanny know about the change, Harry?" His eyes grew big as saucers and he dashed out. In fact, I think the princess did allow them to have pizza that night, and I prepared it with pleasure. The boys also loved American barbeque and every once in a while they could all be found tucked into a booth eating ribs and burgers at a local spot aptly named Sticky Fingers along Kensington High Street.

When I think back, it seems to me that the princess knew her time with her children was a scarce treasure. It would disappear as they grew up and assumed more of their royal responsibilities. She tried to let both of them have as normal and relaxed a childhood as possible, and I think William and Harry really benefited from that. To have complete unconditional love from their mother was a source of strength for them. They were full of energy, inquisitive, courteous, and temperamentally kind. You always knew when they were around: the corridors would be thundering with noise of the boys racing along the hallway or kicking a ball or doing all the things that boys do. It brought the house to life. It brought the princess to life too.

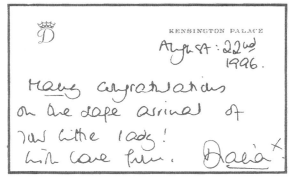

The card sent from Princess Diana when my daughter Kelly was born. It came with the biggest bouquet of flowers I have ever seen.

ENTERTAINING AT HOME

Princess Diana always took an active interest in the world around her. By the time of her death, she was patron of 119 different charities, a huge number. But that was Princess Diana. When she saw a worthwhile cause, she threw herself into it. She didn't have handlers or advisers or any of the BP "gray suits," as she called them, testing the waters and advising her on protocol. The princess was herself, spontaneous and sometimes impetuous. That and her kindness and warmth were her greatest strengths.

She opened her house often to entertain on behalf of the charities she worked so hard for. No dinner parties, though. Lunch only. That was by design.

She was sure that the press would have a field day and there would be no end to the stories of who was in her house at night. But lunch, well, who could gossip about that?

Though the dining room could hold up to thirty comfortably, luncheons were usually limited to twelve. Princess Diana preferred smaller groups. She said that it gave her a chance to talk to everyone around the table. Her entertaining style was formal, but she made everyone relax as soon as they walked through the door. "Look them in the eye and give a firm handshake," was her mantra. The dining room was very feminine with lots of pretty china and flowers. She had it completely repainted after the prince moved out and now the walls were a rustic, but tasteful, burnt orange. No gilt, no under butlers, no stewards and wine waiters, no pomp at all.

Beet Red

The princess liked all different kinds of juice, and so I learned to prepare all sorts, including veggie juices. Once she came into the kitchen and said she had heard beetroot juice was very good for your skin and she would like a glass. I glanced quickly in my juicing book, which mentioned that you should dilute beet juice with carrot or apple. But since she just wanted a shot, I juiced some beets and she drank it down. She had appointments set up all afternoon and wanted to look her best. By midmorning, her skin began to form red splotches and she was having palpitations.

She came racing into the kitchen. "Aargh, Darren!" she cried. "I think you've poisoned me!"

Well, I was pretty sure that she would live to see another day, but I was a bit alarmed. *Good Lord,* I thought, *what did that juice do?* It turned out that the book was right. Beet juice is quite strong and needs to be tempered or diluted with other juices. After a quick stint on a tanning bed, the princess's blotches began to fade and she was able to make her afternoon appointments. I refrained from juicing anything red for a while, though she did laugh when I slyly put beetroot soufflé on the menu the next day.

When she entertained I would try to introduce new dishes to the menu. Some of her favorites were pressed vegetable terrines with a pureed herb dressing, carrot and egg roulade with a maple ginger dressing, baked crabmeat and

Hollywood at Home

Princess Diana once hosted a lunch for the actor Clint Eastwood. I can't remember the exact reason for the lunch, but I do remember that it was only one where I was called into the dining room. It seems Mr. Eastwood had enjoyed his lunch so much he asked to speak to the chef directly. I stepped through the green baize door and was introduced by the princess. Mr. Eastwood stood up to shake my hand and I was surprised at how tall he was! I'm six feet two inches and am usually the tallest one in the room. At six feet four inches, he had me bested by a few inches. I don't recall what he said. I just stood there in utter surprise with a sheepish grin on my face. What can I say except that it "made my day."

corn custards, chicken breast stuffed with red pepper and basil mousse, and iced praline and amaretto soufflés with poached pears.

Some of her old favorites were on the menu too. Tomato mousse with lobster was a dish she loved from her Buckingham Palace days. The original recipe called for three different kinds of fat and she had me rework the recipe into a fat-free version. I remember on one occasion when a famous American talk show host came for lunch and I served the tomato mousse. The princess and I chuckled later when she told me how the guest had gushed: "Diana this is wonderful! How do you manage to stay so slim?" Of course, the guest was eating the original recipe while the boss had the fat-free version.

Of course, if the boys had friends over, then the menu was more kid-friendly: pork loin with apple sauce, poached chicken in a supreme sauce with rice and nursery favorites, baked jam roll and custard or a pear and banana crumble, a Prince Charles favorite.

Over the years, the princess opened her home to all sorts of people, some famous, but many were just regular people doing good work. I remember she once invited a little boy over for lunch. He had cancer and had written to her saying he would very much like to have lunch with a princess. He arrived at Kensington Palace in a black taxicab with his sister and mother in tow. You could tell his mom was nervous. Enough pressure having lunch with a real-life princess, but to have to do it with your kids!

The princess asked me to serve something William and Harry liked to eat, so I roasted two chickens and some vegetables. In the dining room the princess had placed a gift-wrapped toy truck on the little boy's seat, a doll on his sister's, and a hand-tied bouquet of flowers on the table for his mother. They all sat down to eat and the princess did her best to put everyone at ease.

Halfway through the meal the little boy picked up his drumstick with his hands and began gnawing at the bone. The mother had a terrified look on her face and Princess Diana, reading the situation quickly, put down her fork and knife and picked up her chicken with her hands too. The boy's mother smiled and breathed a sigh of relief. That was classic Princess Diana—she never missed a thing.

A COMPLICATED LIFE

I always look back on my years at Kensington with pleasure. I was really happy there. But in all honesty, I don't think that was always true for the princess. She found it extremely hard to have a normal life. The media focus on her was intense. The princess, because of her marriage and her charity work, was a person of interest to every major news and media outlet in the world. And wherever she went, the press followed. The fact that she lived her life in a goldfish bowl made her more adamant that only those people who could guard her privacy were allowed to stay in her house. If she felt you were untrustworthy, you ended up leaving Kensington. She initially had a personal protection officer assigned to her from the palace, but ended up asking him to leave. She felt her every move was reported back to Buckingham Palace, and she just couldn't stand that.

She missed her children all the time. The custody arrangement was that she and Prince Charles would each have the boys on alternate free weekends and alternate holidays. By the time that Prince Charles and Princess Diana had separated, both William and Harry were in boarding school and most weekends they stayed at school. That was hard on her. She was not yet ready for them to be away so much. And while she and the Prince split custody of the children

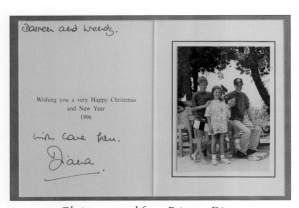

Christmas card from Princess Diana

on holidays, Princess Diana never celebrated Christmas with her children. She felt that at Christmas, the rightful place for the boys was at Sandringham with the rest of the royal family. It was a tradition she was willing to support, but it left her in tears and with a big hole in her Christmas holiday. She was alone then; all the staff were away visiting their own families. I would load up the refrigerator with goodies for her and head out of the door on Christmas Eve.

Cufflinks given to me by Princess Diana

Dating was difficult for her and she could be fickle in her affections. She didn't have a clear sense about what she wanted her love life to be. It was a work in progress, impeded by the relentless attention her every move generated. She was really pleased at my own good fortune in meeting my wife. She thought it must be blissfully easy to form relationships when your life wasn't so public. I think she was absolutely right.

There is no doubt she had her faults. The princess was neither a martyr nor a saint. She could get furious at someone for a perceived slight and then never speak to that person again. She stopped speaking to me for a few days after I drove too fast into work one day, nearly colliding with her car as she headed out to the gym. My apologies were profuse, but not enough to stop her from telling the rest of the staff that I had nearly killed her. Fortunately for me, after a few days all was forgiven.

Princess Diana was a woman building a new life and sometimes its outlines were not clear to her. She could feel lost. I was her chef and she often sat in the kitchen eating her lunch and chatting. Sometimes the conversation was just about what happened in last night's soap operas and other times she would burst in and say, "Darren, you won't believe what the Queen [or often Fergie] has just told me!" If she trusted you, then you were privy to everything and anything on her mind. Conversations would meander over topics, covering a little bit of this and that. Listening to her I felt that her innate compassion and kindness would help her mature into a woman of great purpose. She just needed time to grow into it, as we all do.

I didn't know that time was the one thing she didn't have.

I woke up early on Sunday, August 31, 1997. It was going to be a fun day. The "boss" was flying back from her vacation, and William and Harry would be at the house for a few days before they went back to school. The boys had been at Balmoral and were flying in to the VIP terminal at about the same time as the princess. They'd all be at Kensington for dinner and I had already bought the food.

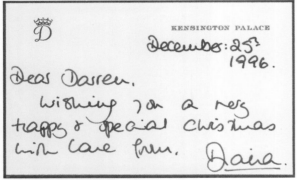

This note card accompanied a Hermes tie on Christmas Eve. It was to be the last gift I received from the princess before she died.

I sat down to breakfast and flipped the television on. I heard the BBC newscaster mention Princess Diana, but it took me several seconds to make any sense of what he was saying. Onscreen flashed a picture of the princess with the dates July 1, 1961–August 31, 1997 underneath. What was he talking about? He couldn't be right. Her Royal Highness dead? No, there must be a mistake. I called Kensington Palace but only got a constant busy signal.

I decided to go in to work, taking all the food I had bought for dinner with me. As I drove through the gate into the royal compound, the usually cheery police officer acknowledged me, then quickly looked away. I parked my car and headed to the apartment, passing the princess's office as I did. The office door was open and I stepped inside. Several staff mates were there, some in tears. No one said anything. We all just stood there, none of us really believing what had happened. The fax machine suddenly broke the silence.

"Oh my God!" I heard one of the secretaries say. "It is the princess's last will and testament." The fax was from Antony Julius, the princess's attorney. It was then that I realized she wasn't coming home.

During the next week I went in to work each day and cooked meals for anyone who was around. No one ate anything. Not even me. Instead I took to ambling around Kensington Palace gardens where only weeks before the princess had gone walking or roller-blading in a baseball cap and dark glasses so as not to be recognized.

The park was now jammed full of people, all in mourning. Bouquets of flowers, stacked almost three feet high, were piled against the black and gilt palace railings, and the perfume brought back memories of the princess's birthday each year

Signed Photo of Princess Diana in gilt frame with Prince of Wales feathers

when it seemed like every five minutes another bouquet was delivered to the house from a charity, a friend, an admirer, or just from someone whose life she had touched, someone she didn't even know. I noticed that many of the bouquets were freesias, her favorite flower. Candles lit up the park and I remembered how much she loved candlelight. The apartment often carried the scent of Kenneth Turner original fragrance candles. She had given me one as a Christmas gift. I still have it and light it on special occasions.

The days preceding the funeral went by in slow motion. I was out of sorts. I didn't want to cook and instead ate at McDonald's six nights in a row. It was familiar and anonymous and oddly comforting. Along with the rest of the household staff, I was allowed to visit the princess in the chapel, pay my last respects, and sign the condolence book.

On the day of the funeral we were all at Kensington Palace by nine in the morning. We formed a line at the front door, as we often did when Princess Diana went off on a long journey, this time to say good-bye for the last time. We were whisked to Westminster Abbey, through streets lined with more than a million people. The funeral was difficult for me. I sat directly across from Elton John as he sang "Candle in the Wind" in tribute to the princess. I felt a lump in my throat that became tears as her brother, Earl Spencer, gave the eulogy.

It wasn't until I was driving home that evening that I suddenly thought, *Now what am I going to do with myself?* I stopped at McDonald's for a burger and time to think. I had been told that I'd stay on the payroll for six months and the princess's sisters had requested that I keep my grace and favor accommodation for up to a year and not be turned out onto the streets. Good. That would give me time to sort out my next move.

Mohammed Al Fayed, Dodi's father, had promised jobs to any members of the princess's staff, if they wanted one. But I hadn't really thought about that. Prince

Knowing how much the princess adored her father, I sent her a note when he passed away. I didn't expect a reply, but the princess loved to write notes.

Charles also offered me a position as a personal chef, but I declined. I think I would have forever felt Princess Diana looking down on me saying, "You are not going to cook for that woman, are you?" I was also offered a position with Michael Hesseltine, the former deputy prime minister, at his stately home in Oxfordshire, but he and I were politically poles apart. I decided that wouldn't work.

The princess had always talked about moving to America. After every visit to the States she would come into the kitchen and say, "Darren, we've absolutely got to move there!"

I would just laugh and reply, "Just give me time to pack a few clothes and the juicer, your Royal Highness." I called her "your Royal Highness" right up until her death, despite the removal of the title after the divorce. I don't know. It didn't seem right to call her by any lesser title.

During the next weeks my thoughts kept turning back to those conversations. *America. Live in America. Well, someone must need a chef there. I could find someplace warm. Definitely someplace warm and away from all of this. Maybe that just might work . . .*

CARROT AND EGG ROULADE WITH MESCLUN SALAD AND A MAPLE GINGER DRESSING

This is a versatile dish that can be made several days ahead. I would make this on a Friday morning and refrigerate it for the princess to eat over the weekend. It is soft enough to spoon onto a plate so that you don't have to slice it. Sometimes I would use a cookie cutter and cut disks out of the baked roulade and make Napoleons, using the egg mixture as the filling. Tarragon, dill, and even cilantro can be used interchangeably in this recipe.

Roulade

1/2	stick (1/4 cup) unsalted butter
1 1/2	pounds carrots, finely grated
6	eggs, separated
2	tablespoons chopped fresh tarragon
	Salt and freshly ground pepper

Filling

6	hard-boiled eggs, chopped
2	tablespoons finely chopped fresh dill
2	ribs celery, finely chopped
1/4	teaspoon celery seeds
1	cup mayonnaise
	Salt and freshly ground pepper

Dressing

1/4	cup olive oil
2	tablespoons maple syrup
1 1/2	tablespoons sherry vinegar
1	tablespoon lemon juice
1/2	teaspoon ground cinnamon
1/4	teaspoon ground nutmeg
1	teaspoon ground ginger
1	pound mesclun (gourmet salad mix), rinsed and dried

1. Preheat the oven to 400 degrees.

2. **For the roulade**, line an 12 x 8-inch pan with parchment paper. Melt the butter in a sauté pan until foaming; then add the carrots, and cook gently until soft. Let the mixture cool in a separate bowl. Add the egg yolks and tarragon, and season with salt and pepper to taste. Stir to combine. In a separate bowl, whisk the egg whites until stiff, and fold them into the carrot mixture. Pour into the prepared tin, and bake for 10 minutes, or slightly longer, until it is golden brown on top and springy to the touch. Remove from the oven and invert onto a large sheet of parchment paper. Peel off the original layer of parchment to allow the steam to escape and the roulade to cool.

3. **For the filling**, mix the eggs, dill, celery, and celery seeds with the mayonnaise. Season with salt and pepper to taste. Spread the filling on top of the roulade, leaving a 1/2-inch border all around the edges. Using the fresh parchment paper as an aid, roll up the roulade from one end to the other. Trim the edges.

4. **For the dressing**, whisk together the olive oil, maple syrup, sherry, lemon juice, cinnamon, nutmeg, and ginger, and taste for seasoning. Pour over the mesclun and toss. To serve, slice the roulade into equal pieces. Place a slice on a plate with the salad. Accompany the salad with warm crusty rolls.

MAKES 8 SERVINGS

AVOCADO AND HEARTS OF PALM SALAD

1	head Bibb or butterhead lettuce	2	teaspoons sugar
1	(16-ounce) jar hearts of palm rings, drained	1	teaspoon Dijon mustard
1	ripe avocado, diced	2	teaspoons lemon juice
2	navel oranges, peeled and segmented	1	tablespoon walnut oil
1	small red bell pepper, finely diced	1/4	cup water
1/2	small red onion, finely diced		Salt and freshly ground pepper
1/4	cup raspberry vinegar	1	tablespoon chopped fresh tarragon

1. Tear the lettuce leaves into bite-size pieces, removing the center rib of the outer leaves. Place the lettuce in a large bowl. Add the hearts of palm, avocado, orange segments, bell pepper, and red onion.

2. Blend the raspberry vinegar, sugar, mustard, lemon juice, walnut oil, and water together. Season to taste with the salt and pepper. Fold in the tarragon. Drizzle 2 tablespoons of the dressing over the salad, and divide the salad among four plates. Drizzle each plate with more dressing. Serve immediately.

MAKES 4 SERVINGS

FALL GREENS WITH ROASTED BEETS, CARAMELIZED WALNUTS, AND GOAT CHEESE WITH WALNUT DRESSING

1	pound fresh beets, about 3 small
¼	cup walnuts
1	tablespoon sugar
3	tablespoons plus 1 teaspoon corn oil
2	tablespoons white wine vinegar
1	teaspoon Dijon mustard
3	tablespoons walnut oil
1	teaspoon water

	Salt and freshly ground pepper
1	6-ounce bag mixed salad leaves
4	ounces soft goat cheese, crumbled
4	slices center-cut bacon, broiled until crispy and finely chopped
1	Gala apple, peeled, seeded, and finely diced

1. Preheat the oven to 350 degrees. Trim the leaves off the beets, and scrub the beets clean of any dirt or grit. Wrap the beets in aluminum foil and bake for 1 hour, or until fork tender. Remove from the oven and allow to cool. Peel, then cut, the beets into cubes and place them in a small bowl.

2. Place the walnuts, sugar, and 1 teaspoon corn oil in a heavy pan over high heat, and stir until the sugar caramelizes and the walnuts darken slightly. Turn the nuts out onto a lightly greased plate.

3. In a large bowl whisk together the white wine vinegar, mustard, the remaining 3 tablespoons corn oil, the walnut oil, and water. Season with the salt and pepper to taste, and pour half the mixture over the beets to marinate for about 30 minutes.

4. Divide the salad leaves among four plates, and arrange the beets, goat cheese, bacon, and apples on top. Drizzle the salad with the remaining dressing to taste. Sprinkle on the walnuts and serve.

MAKES 4 SERVINGS

PRESSED VEGETABLE TERRINE

1 head fennel, bulb only
1 large red bell pepper
¼ cup olive oil
1 teaspoon oregano
 Salt and freshly ground pepper
4 ounces mozzarella cheese, sliced into ¼-inch slices and cut into disks to fit the ramekins
2 tablespoons extra virgin olive oil

1 pinch of red pepper flakes
1 clove garlic, crushed
1 (5-ounce) block Boursin cheese
2 large ripe tomatoes, quartered, skinned, and seeded
1 (4-ounce) bag mesclun (mixed salad leaves)
 Puréed Herb Dressing (Page 215)

1. Preheat the oven to 400 degrees. Slice the fennel bulb lengthwise into ½-inch slices. Cut the bell pepper lengthwise into four pieces, discarding the seeds. Lay the fennel and bell pepper on a baking sheet, drizzle with the olive oil, and then sprinkle with the oregano, and salt and pepper to taste. Bake until tender, about 15 minutes.

2. Prepare the marinade for the mozzarella by mixing the extra virgin olive oil with the red pepper flakes, garlic, and salt and pepper to taste in a small bowl. Add the mozzarella slices, and marinate them for at least 1 hour.

3. Line four 5-ounce ramekins with plastic wrap and start building the terrine in layers. Start with the red bell pepper, cut into a disc to fit into the bottom of the ramekin. Save the pepper trimmings to be used as the last layer on the terrine. Next add a scant tablespoon of the Boursin, followed by a piece of roasted fennel, mozzarella, and tomato. Divide the remaining Boursin among the ramekins, and finish with the pepper trimmings.

4. Wrap the terrines tightly, and put weights on the top. Refrigerate, weighted down, for at least 24 hours.

5. Turn each terrine out onto a plate, and allow the terrines to come to room temperature before serving. Garnish with the salad leaves and pureéd herb dressing.

MAKES 4 SERVINGS

PARSNIP AND APPLE SOUP WITH PARMESAN-CHIVE FOAM

This recipe, which I often prepared for the princess, has the right balance between silky, earthy parsnip flavor and the taste of tart/sweet apple that comes through. Make time to prepare the garnish; it turns a good soup into a great one.

Soup

2	tablespoons unsalted butter
1	pound parsnips, peeled and chopped
1	Granny Smith apple, peeled and chopped
1	medium onion, peeled and chopped
1	teaspoon ground coriander
3	cups water
1	chicken bouillon cube
1/2	cup heavy cream
	Salt and freshly ground black pepper

Garnish

1/4	cup heavy cream
1	tablespoon freshly grated Parmesan
3	tablespoons roughly chopped fresh chives, divided
1	Granny Smith apple, peeled

1. **For the soup**, melt the butter in a heavy-bottomed saucepan. When the butter has stopped foaming, add the parsnips, apple, and onion. Sauté until the onion is translucent and soft, about 5 minutes. Add the coriander, water, and bouillon cube. Bring the soup up to a gentle simmer, turn down the heat, and simmer until the parsnips are tender enough to be easily pierced with a fork. Remove the soup from the heat and with a hand-held blender, puree the soup. If you want to use a standard blender to puree the soup, you will need to let the soup cool down before blending. After blending the soup, strain the contents through a fine-mesh strainer to remove any lumps. The soup can be made ahead up to this point and refrigerated for several days. Warm gently before continuing.

2. Stir in the cream, and season to taste with the salt and pepper. Let the soup get hot, but do not boil. Adjust the consistency, thinning with a little water if needed.

3. **For the garnish**, whip the heavy cream until stiff peaks form. Fold the Parmesan and 1 tablespoon of the chives into the whipped cream. Grate some of the apple into the bottom of four warm soup bowls, and ladle the soup on top. Spoon the Parmesan cream on top of the soup, and garnish with the remaining 2 tablespoons chives.

MAKES 4 SERVINGS

*Parsnip and Apple Soup, Pear and Walnut Salad with
Parmesan Balsamic Dressing*

STUFFED BELL PEPPERS

4	medium red bell peppers		1	cup rice, cooked until al dente and cooled
1/4	cup olive oil		1/2	cup water
1/2	cup roughly chopped onion		1/2	chicken or vegetable bouillon cube
1	cup finely sliced button mushrooms		4	slices smoked bacon, broiled crispy and chopped
1	zucchini, diced		1	tablespoon fresh basil, shredded
1/2	teaspoon dried oregano		4	ounces mozzarella cheese, diced
	Salt and freshly ground pepper		2	tablespoons grated Parmesan cheese
2	tomatoes, roughly chopped			

1. Preheat the oven to 350 degrees. Cut the tops off the peppers, and clean out the seeds and membranes. If the peppers won't stand up, cut a little piece off the bottom to level them. Place the peppers on a baking sheet, and drizzle with the oil. Bake for 25 minutes, or until they start to soften. Remove from the oven and allow to cool.

2. Pour the oil from the peppers into a frying pan, and add the onions, mushrooms, zucchini, and oregano. Season the vegetables with the salt and pepper to taste, and sauté over high heat until they start to soften. Add the tomatoes, rice, water, and bouillon cube, and simmer for about 5 minutes. Adjust the seasoning.

3. Fold in the bacon, basil, and mozzarella, and divide among the peppers. Sprinkle the Parmesan on top of the peppers, and bake in the middle of the oven for 15 minutes, or until the cheese has melted and the filling is hot.

MAKES 4 SERVINGS.

Stuffed Bell Peppers, Stuffed Aubergine (Stuffed Egglplant)

Spinach and Red Pepper Roulade with Shaved Parmesan

2	tablespoons unsalted butter, for greasing

Filling

2	red bell peppers, cut in half lengthwise
2	sprigs fresh rosemary, cut in half
1	small clove garlic, crushed
1	teaspoon olive oil
8	ounces cream cheese
1	egg yolk
	Salt and freshly ground pepper

Roulade

1	tablespoon olive oil
1	cup sliced button mushrooms
1	(20-ounce) bag spinach leaves
3	egg yolks
1	small bunch of fresh chives, finely chopped
	Salt and freshly ground pepper
4	egg whites
1	cup finely grated Parmesan cheese

1. Preheat the oven to 350 degrees. Grease a 13 x 9-inch baking sheet, line it with parchment paper, and grease the parchment paper.

2. **For the filling,** place the red pepper halves in a shallow roasting pan with a piece of rosemary, some garlic, and olive oil in each cavity of the pepper. Roast the peppers in the oven for 30 to 40 minutes, or until the peppers start to soften. Remove from the oven, and put in a ziplock bag or a bowl covered with plastic to steam the peppers. When the peppers get to room temperature, peel off the skins, and discard the rosemary. Put the red peppers into a blender, and blend them finely. Add the cream cheese and egg yolk, and continue blending. Season with the salt and pepper to taste.

3. **For the roulade,** heat the olive oil in a large frying pan, and add the mushrooms, stirring until they start to soften. Add the spinach to the mushrooms, and stir until the spinach leaves start to wilt. Remove the pan from the heat and allow the spinach mix to cool. Fold in the egg yolks and chives, and season with salt and pepper.

4. Whisk the egg whites until stiff, and fold them into the spinach mixture. Spread the mixture evenly onto a baking sheet, and bake for 15 minutes, or until just firm to the touch.

5. Lay a sheet of parchment paper out on the table, and sprinkle the grated Parmesan cheese onto it. When the roulade is cooked, remove from the oven, and turn it onto the prepared parchment. Trim the edges off the roulade. Spread the red pepper filling evenly across the roulade, taking care to leave about a 1/2-inch border around the

edges. Holding the parchment paper, roll up the roulade, squeezing it gently as you go so it rolls up to a nice round shape. Slice into thick slices, and return them, on their sides, to the oven for 5 more minutes until they are warm. You can also prepare them up to this stage in advance, and cool them in the refrigerator. If so, they'll need to bake about 10 minutes to completely heat through.

6. Serve the roulade in place of a vegetable side dish. You can also serve it as a main course, as I used to do for Princess Diana, on a bed of salad leaves tossed in olive oil and lemon juice with toasted walnut pieces and shaved Parmesan as garnish.

MAKES 6 SERVINGS

PEAR AND WALNUT SALAD WITH PARMESAN BALSAMIC DRESSING

Dressing

- 1/2 cup olive oil
- 1/4 cup fresh Parmesan cheese
- 3 tablespoons minced fresh basil
- 1 teaspoon lemon juice
- 2 tablespoons balsamic vinegar
- 1 clove garlic, crushed
  Salt and freshly ground pepper

Salad

- 1 head butter lettuce
- 1 teaspoon lemon juice
- 1 teaspoon olive oil
- 1 ripe pear, peeled and sliced
- 4 ounces goat cheese, crumbled
- 3 tablespoons roughly chopped walnuts, toasted
- 1 green onion, finely chopped

1. **For the dressing**, mix together the oil, Parmesan, basil, lemon juice, vinegar, garlic, and salt and pepper to taste. Shake or whisk to blend. Refrigerate for up to three days.

2. **For the salad,** wash and tear the lettuce into bite-size pieces, discarding the outer leaves. Add the lemon juice and olive oil, and toss. Divide the lettuce among six salad plates, and arrange the pear slices, goat cheese, walnuts, and green onion on top. Drizzle the dressing over the salad and around the edges of the plate. Serve immediately.

MAKES 6 SERVINGS

LOBSTER THERMIDOR

1   stick (½ cup) unsalted butter, divided
¼   cup all-purpose flour
1   cup milk
1   cup plus 2 tablespoons heavy cream
2   (1½-pound) lobsters, cooked and cooled
½   cup finely chopped onions

¼   cup brandy
1   cup grated Gruyère cheese
1   teaspoon Dijon mustard
     Salt and reshly ground pepper
2   egg yolks, beaten
4   tablespoons grated Parmesan cheese
2   tablespoons chopped fresh chives

1. Preheat the broiler to high, and place a shelf in the top part of the oven. In a heavy saucepan, add ¼ cup butter and the flour. Stir until the butter melts and the flour is incorporated. Reduce the heat to low, and gradually whisk in the milk and 1 cup cream until combined and no lumps appear. Simmer for 10 minutes, stirring occasionally.

2. Cut the lobster in half down the middle, and remove the meat from the tail and claws. Remove the vein from the center of the tail and discard it. Cut the lobster meat into bite-size pieces. Clean out the four shell halves, but keep them intact, and place them on a small baking sheet.

3. In a frying pan, melt the remaining ¼ cup butter, and add the finely chopped onions. Sauté the onions until soft and translucent. Add the brandy and then the lobster meat, and sauté until warm.

4. Add the Gruyère cheese and mustard to the thick cream sauce, and stir to combine. Season with the salt and pepper to taste. Remove the sauce from the heat. Mix the yolks with the remaining 2 tablespoons heavy cream and stir into the sauce. Spoon a little of the sauce into the bottom of each shell and divide the lobster meat among the four shells, placing the meat on top of the sauce. Spoon more sauce over the lobster, and sprinkle with the Parmesan cheese. Broil for 3 to 4 minutes, or until hot and golden brown. Sprinkle with the chopped chives, and serve immediately.

MAKES 4 SERVINGS

Lobster Thermidor

SMOKED SALMON AND CRABMEAT CUSTARDS

Custards

1	tablespoon olive oil
1	tablespoon unsalted butter
2	ribs celery, finely chopped
1/2	cup finely chopped red bell pepper
4	eggs
1 1/4	cups milk
1/2	cup heavy cream
2	tablespoons fresh white bread crumbs
1	tablespoon roughly chopped chives
	Salt and freshly ground pepper
8	ounces sliced smoked salmon
4	ounces jumbo lump crabmeat

Salad

1	small head radicchio
1	small head oak leaf lettuce
1	small bunch dill
1	teaspoon olive oil
1/2	lemon, juiced
2	tablespoons prepared horseradish
2	tablespoons sour cream
1/4	cup mayonnaise
1	teaspoon minced garlic
1/4	teaspoon cider vinegar
12	grape tomatoes

1. Preheat the oven to 325 degrees.

2. **For the custards,** melt the oil and butter together in a small skillet over medium heat. Sauté the celery and bell pepper until soft, but not colored. Remove from the heat and allow to cool.

3. In a medium bowl beat the eggs, and whisk in the milk and cream. Add the bread crumbs and the chives. Season with the salt and pepper to taste.

4. Line four ovenproof ramekins with the smoked salmon, so that none of the ramekin shows through. Pick through the crabmeat to discard any shell, and distribute it equally among the four ramekins on top of the salmon.

5. Add the sautéed peppers and celery to the egg mixture, and stir well. Pour it over the crab until it comes up to the top of the smoked salmon lining.

6. Place the ramekins on a baking sheet in the center of the oven for 30 minutes, or until the egg mixture is firm to touch. Remove from the oven, and allow to cool for a few minutes

7. **For the salad and dressing**, tear the radicchio and oak leaf lettuce into fork-size pieces and put them into a large bowl. You can use whatever lettuce you like best, but I feel

that these two complement the salmon custards the best. Tear off sprigs of dill, and add to the lettuce. Toss the lettuce with the olive oil and lemon juice, and split among four plates.

8. In a small bowl combine the horseradish, sour cream, mayonnaise, garlic, and cider vinegar. Carefully remove the salmon custards from the molds, and place them in the center of the plates. Drizzle the horseradish dressing around the lettuce, and garnish with the tomatoes.

MAKES 4 SERVINGS

CHILLED TOMATO AND DILL MOUSSE
(Fat-Free Version)

1	pound vine-ripe tomatoes, chopped	1	packet unflavored gelatin
2	tablespoons chopped onion	1/3	cup fat-free chicken broth
8	ounces fat-free cream cheese, softened	1	teaspoon lemon juice
2	tablespoons fat-free sour cream		Salt and freshly ground pepper
1	tablespoon tomato paste	1	tablespoon chopped fresh dill

1. Put the tomatoes and onions in a food processor, and blend until they become finely blended and somewhat soupy. Strain through a sieve into a large bowl. Discard the remaining seeds and skins. Whisk in the cream cheese, sour cream, and tomato paste until there are no lumps.

2. In a small saucepan, add the gelatin, chicken broth, and lemon juice. Stir until softened, and then warm the saucepan over low heat until the gelatin has dissolved. Whisk the gelatin mixture into the tomato mixture, and season with the salt and pepper to taste.

3. Fold in the dill, and pour the tomato mousse into six ramekins. Refrigerate uncovered for at least 2 hours. Serve in the ramekins, or dip the ramekins in hot water, run a knife around the edge of the molds, and invert onto the plates.

MAKES 6 SERVINGS

STUFFED AUBERGINE
(Stuffed Eggplant)

This dish brings back fond memories of my days in the Princess of Wales's kitchen. Stuffed Aubergine, known as eggplant to American cooks, was one of the princess's favorite dishes. More often than not, she'd request that I leave an extra serving in the refrigerator for her to reheat on the weekend. That was all right; this is one of those dishes that seems to improve with age and can be prepared ahead of time. The flavors and textures create a healthy and great-tasting lunch when served alone with a salad, or as a vegetable side dish served alongside a grilled steak.

2	small eggplants, each 6-inches long	1½	cups sliced button mushrooms
4	tablespoons olive oil, divided	1	large tomato, finely chopped
1	large zucchini	2	slices bacon, cooked until crisp
1	large orange bell pepper	1	cup grated mozzarella cheese
2	ribs celery	1	tablespoon chopped fresh basil
½	cup roughly chopped red onion	2	tablespoons grated Parmesan cheese
	Salt and freshly ground pepper		

1. Preheat the oven to 350 degrees.

2. Cut each eggplant in half into two equal cylinders. Cut a circle in the white flesh of the eggplants about ¼ inch from the skin all the way round, and about 1 inch deep. Score the inside of the circle (i.e., make tiny cross-cuts into the flesh of the circle about ½ inch deep). This makes it easier to scoop out the flesh once the eggplant is cooked.

3. Brush the eggplants with 2 tablespoons olive oil, especially the cut top and bottom, and bake on a tray in the oven for 15 to 20 minutes. Turn each eggplant over midway through cooking so the bottoms don't get too brown. When the flesh feels soft, remove the eggplants from the oven, and allow them to cool.

4. Coarsely chop the zucchini, bell pepper, and celery into ¾-inch cubes. In a skillet, put 2 tablespoons olive oil on medium heat. Add the zucchini, bell pepper, celery, red onion, and mushrooms. Season with salt and pepper, and cook until the vegetables start to soften. Stir in the tomato, taste, adjust seasoning, and allow the mixture to cool.

5. Finely chop the bacon, dice the mozzarella into small cubes, and add these to the cooled vegetables along with the chopped basil.

6. Gently remove the flesh from the insides of the eggplant, taking care to leave about ¼ inch on the bottom to create a shell. Then chop the flesh, and add it to the vegetables. Spoon the mix into the eggplant shells, dividing it among the four. Sprinkle the tops with the Parmesan cheese.

7. The stuffed eggplants are now ready, and they can be placed in the oven for 15 minutes, or until the filling is hot. Or they can be refrigerated, ready for a princess to reheat straight from the refrigerator to oven. Serve with a salad or as a vegetable.

MAKES 4 SERVINGS

PUREED HERB DRESSING

2	cups mixed fresh herbs (dill, chives, basil, tarragon, parsley)
6	tablespoons white balsamic vinegar
6	tablespoons extra virgin olive oil
2	tablespoons chopped onions
1	tablespoon sugar
	Salt and freshly ground pepper

Combine all ingredients and blend in a food processor or blender until smooth. Adjust seasoning with salt and pepper. Wait one hour before serving to allow the flavors to fully infuse the oil. Can be refrigerated for up to three days.

MAKES 6 SERVINGS

POACHED EGGS SUZETTE

2 large russet potatoes, about 12 ounces each

2 tablespoons unsalted butter plus 3 tablespoons butter, melted

3 egg yolks, divided

Salt and freshly ground pepper

1 teaspoon lemon juice

1 teaspoon olive oil

2 cups spinach leaves, firmly packed

1 pinch grated nutmeg

1 teaspoon white wine vinegar

1 teaspoon salt

2 large eggs

1 teaspoon chopped fresh tarragon

1. Preheat the oven to 400 degrees, and place a rack in the middle. Bake the potatoes for 1 hour or longer, until slightly soft to the touch. Remove the potatoes and slice one-fourth off the top of the potatoes lengthways. Scoop out the flesh from the potato into a large bowl. Put the potato shells onto a baking sheet.

2. Mash the potatoes until smooth, adding 2 tablespoons butter, 1 egg yolk, and salt and pepper to taste. Using a piping bag fitted with a star tip, pipe the potatoes around the top of the potato shells, and return to the oven for 15 minutes, or until golden brown. Prepare the filling while the potatoes are browning.

3. For the filling, place the remaining 2 egg yolks into a metal bowl, or the top part of a double boiler, over a pan of boiling water. Whisk the yolks, and gradually add the lemon juice and the remaining 3 tablespoons melted butter. Season with salt and pepper to taste, set aside, and keep warm.

4. Heat the olive oil in a frying pan, and add the spinach. Sauté the spinach until it wilts, and add the nutmeg and the salt and pepper to taste. Divide the spinach between the two potato shells, and keep them warm.

5. Bring a 2-quart pan of water to a boil, add the vinegar, and the 1 teaspoon salt. Carefully poach the eggs for about 3 minutes. Remove them with a slotted spoon, and place on top of the spinach in the potato shells.

6. Spoon the sauce over each egg and sprinkle with the chopped tarragon. Serve immediately.

MAKES 2 SERVINGS

PEACH PANNA COTTA

1	packet unflavored gelatin	3	ripe peaches
2¼	cups heavy cream, divided	1	tablespoon vanilla sugar (see page 76)
⅓	cup plus 1 tablespoon sugar	1	teaspoon roughly chopped fresh mint
¼	teaspoon vanilla paste	6	individual ramekins
½	cup eau de vie de peches (peach brandy)		

1. Soften the gelatin in ¼ cup heavy cream in a bowl. Bring the remaining 2 cups heavy cream and the sugar to a simmer in a large saucepan set over high heat. Remove the pan from the heat, add the gelatin mix to the hot cream, and whisk together until the gelatin and sugar are fully dissolved. Add the vanilla paste and peach brandy. Strain the mixture into six individual ramekins. Refrigerate overnight, or until set.

2. Stone and peel the peaches, and dice into ¼-inch pieces. Place the peaches in a bowl, add the vanilla sugar and mint, and mix gently.

3. Unmold each panna cotta onto a dessert plate, and garnish with the fresh peaches.

MAKES 6 SERVINGS